FINGERFOOD
BEST-EVER SMALL FOOD RECIPES

FINGERFOOD
BEST-EVER SMALL FOOD RECIPES

bay books

MEAL PLANNER

Use the following table to plan your best-ever Fingerfood selection. The recipes have been grouped into appropriate classifications and the portion size of each recipe is clearly shown. Plan your menu and then turn to the appropriate page to find your clear and concise recipe together with a large-format picture of the finished dish.

BEEF LAMB & PORK

RECIPE	PAGE	PORTIONS
Oregano and prosciutto pinwheels	18	40
Mini scones with ham, leek and port figs	61	40
Beef en croute with bearnaise	62	40
Spicy koftas	66	45
Cucumber cups with Thai beef salad	81	24
Pork san choy bau	82	25
Beef nachos	98	4
Steamed pork buns	107	24

CHICKEN

RECIPE	PAGE	PORTIONS
Chicken tikka	34	10 skewers
Pumpkin and pesto chicken in filo pastry	42	4
Thai chicken meatballs	46	6 serves
Chicken kebabs with curry mayonnaise	93	4 serves
Chicken san choy bau	125	36
Thai chicken sausage rolls	130	24
Chicken falalfel with tabbouli cones	161	24
Coconut rice in banana leaves	186	12

RICE PULSES & VEGETABLES

RECIPE	PAGE	PORTIONS
Suppli	22	30
Linseed crackers	25	24
Falalfel	26	30

RECIPE	PAGE	PORTIONS
Arancini	114	10
Stuffed mushrooms	117	30
Mexican meatballs	133	28
Sesame beef skewers	146	24
Cornish pasties	149	6
Corned beef, parsnip and mint patties	150	24
Chipolata sausages with horseradish cream	158	12
Baguette with egg, dill pesto and prosciutto	165	30
Toasted figs in prosciutto	169	24
Turkish pizza	178	24

RECIPE	PAGE	PORTIONS
Crunchy wedges	38	48
Bocconcino tomato skewers	41	20
Curried nuts	45	4 1/2 cups
Baby squash with rice stuffing	97	24
Cabbage rolls	100	12 rolls
Mexican bites	104	36
Lentil patties with cumin skordalia	134	32
Sticky rice pockets	181	20

SEAFOOD

RECIPE	PAGE	PORTIONS
Stuffed sardines	21	16
Cucumber and salmon bites	49	40
Cocktail tartlets	50	30

VEGETARIAN

Finger food is ideal for many occasions. You might invite a small group of friends round for hors d'oeuvres before an evening out, or a late supper after going out, or perhaps you are having a special dinner party and want to hand round some canapés with the drinks beforehand. Alternatively, you might be hosting a wild party for 50 people, a marquee wedding for 250 or a simple picnic or brunch in your back garden. Finger food has its place at all these events.

PLANNING A MENU

Many factors will affect your choice of menu. What type of gathering are you intending to have? How long will it go on for? What time of day? What time of year? How many people will be attending? What are their tastes in food? What are their ages and interests? Are there many vegetarians, or seafood-haters? How much time will you have to prepare? How well-equipped is your kitchen?

With finger food it is best to keep it simple. Don't try to attempt too much. A few platters of well-chosen ideas will create more impact and give you more time and freedom than attempting 20 recipes with just small quantities of each. Simply double or treble the recipe quantities given, if necessary, and pile your platters high. If your guests are staying for the whole evening you might want to consider one or two sweet dishes to be brought out later on. The time of day and year will influence you in your choice of hot and cold dishes—in summer there is little need to serve hot dishes, so you'll immediately give yourself more time on the day if you don't need to be cooking and reheating right up until when your guests arrive.

Obviously your choice of guests will have a major bearing on your choice of menu. A gathering of the local football team is probably not going to be fully satisfied by a plate of party quiches and petits fours, while your Great Aunt Maud might be a little perplexed by a selection of Mexican corn dogs and stuffed chillies for her ninetieth birthday. You will have to make your own decisions here. However, a good rule of thumb with a mixed group is to serve a couple of conservative 'all-rounder' items such as quiches or tartlets, something more substantial and usually bread based (especially if you are serving alcohol) and perhaps one or two more innovative ideas. You will find with finger food that people are much more adventurous in their tastes when only a couple of mouthfuls are involved (so perhaps Aunt Maud might enjoy that chilli anyway).

Think about the variety of dishes that you're offering. Try not to repeat ingredients—so don't serve prawn dumplings and prawn tempura (unless you're having an evening for local fishermen with a prawn theme). Think about

the colours and textures and try to get a good, show-stopping variety of both. Think about complementary flavours—sour, salty, spicy, subtle, savoury, sweet, as well as hot and cold—and try to create an interesting balance.

HOW MUCH TO SERVE

One of the biggest quandaries people have when preparing finger food is how much to make. How do you know how many of those little pieces everyone will eat? How do you know which will be the most popular? And what happens if you run out of food?

You will find that most of our recipe serving quantities are given as 'makes 40' for single items such as tarts or pikelets, or 'makes about 20 pieces' to give you an idea of how generously something like a frittata or pizza should be cut. However, some recipes (such as carpaccio or other antipasto dishes) are impossible to calculate in pieces and you will find the recipe states, say, 'serves 8'. By this we mean it will give 8 people one serving as part of a whole antipasto platter.

A rough idea for quantities for pre-dinner nibbles is to serve about 3–5 pieces per person, and for a short (say two to three hour) cocktail party you should allow about 4–6 pieces of food per hour for each person, for as long as the party is expected to continue. For a full-length party or occasion when finger food is being served in place of a sit-down meal (such as a wedding or birthday party), allow 8–12 pieces per person.

Chips and nuts and other stand-bys are not included in this calculation.

As far as variety goes, it's best to keep it simple and concentrate on a few fabulous dishes than have a vast quantity of mediocre ones. We advise for 10–20 people, preparing about six different dishes and, for any number higher than that, about eight dishes.

For a whole evening occasion, you would move through light canapés, to more substantial bites (this is when you would serve any hot dishes) and finish with sweet nibbles.

It is always sensible to give your guests a rough idea of what to expect, food-wise, when you issue the invite. So if you're planning to have a two-hour cocktail party, it's a good idea to put start and (assumed) finish times on the invitation: that way people will be expecting nibbles, not a full meal. If it's an all evening affair, let them know you'll be providing food equivalent to an evening meal. Obviously it's better to make too much food than have people leave feeling hungry.

BUFFET TABLE OR 'WAITER'?

Once you've decided what to serve, you need to decide how you are going to serve it. Once again you will be governed by how many people are attending and how much room and equipment you have available. If you are just

having a few friends over, you will probably be quite happy to hand round the food yourself (or perhaps enlist a couple of friends to help). For a larger gathering you might decide to set up a buffet table, or even to hire waiting staff—either of these options obviously gives you much more freedom on the day.

If you are handing food round, whether you are providing plates or not, make sure to always have plenty of napkins handy. If you aren't providing plates, make sure there's somewhere for people to get rid of used cocktail sticks etc.

If you are using a buffet table, you will need to give its layout some thought. For a large gathering, if you have the space and tables, it is a good idea to set up two tables so that everyone isn't queuing together. If this isn't possible, set up your one table with duplicate dishes starting from each end so that people work from both sides. Have plates, forks, napkins etc. available at each end and, if you are serving sweet food, set it up on a separate table.

The whole idea is not to create a traffic jam. So don't set the buffet table right next to the drinks table or people will get under each other's feet. And, rather than making a general announcement that the food is served, you might want to gradually invite people over to the table in smaller groups. Once again, make sure there is somewhere for people to leave their dirty plates.

PRESENTATION

There is little point in creating wonderful food if you're then going to cram it messily on unsuitable plates or in baskets so that the whole impact is lost. Finger food should always look fabulously tantalizing, so presentation is important. Decorate the platter before arranging the food on top. A beautiful folded napkin, banana leaves or even grape leaves and sprigs of various fresh herbs all make good 'beds' for finger food. Linen napkins look better than paper doilies which can soak up grease and look off-putting when the plate is half empty.

You could also experiment with flat baskets, bowls, steel or glass platters, tiles and wooden boards. The ideas are endless, as long as they are clean and hygienic. Think about the theme of your food when choosing your platters—Tapas and Meze can look stunning served on Mediterranean-style tiles.

Don't mix more than two items on a platter. If you pile your platter high with just one recipe you'll give it great impact, as well as making it much easier to top up when supplies run low. Garnishes should be fresh and small enough not to overshadow the main item.

BEING PREPARED

Choose some foods that can be prepared well ahead and frozen, some that can be made a couple of days in advance and refrigerated, and one or two that need to be finished on the day. At the end of many of our recipes you'll find an 'in advance' note that lets you know what can be done. Limit those to be made on the day to simply frying or baking or to simple garnishing. Last minute cooking should be avoided wherever possible. Cook earlier in the day and reheat just before serving.

Write a detailed list of what you need to buy, what can be prepared in advance and when you should do it. Non-perishable foods can be bought well ahead, while some foods such as fresh herbs and vegetables should be bought as close as possible to the day.

When freezing small items such as mini quiches, meatballs and pikelets, allow them to cool completely before placing on baking paper covered trays and freezing until firm. Then remove from the trays and transfer to freezer bags. Label and seal, pressing out as much air from the bag as possible. Alternatively, arrange in single layers between sheets of greaseproof paper in airtight containers, then seal and freeze. Marinated foods can be frozen in the marinade in plastic bags. Flatten the bag, excluding most of the air and freeze while flat—this will take less time to thaw out.

People often forget to to take a good look at the adequacy of their kitchen equipment. Check that your fridge and freezer are large enough to store all you have planned. Is your oven adequate to reheat large quantities of food? Do you have enough platters, plates, glasses and cutlery? If you don't, all is not lost. These can be easily hired or borrowed. Just don't forget to check beforehand and be prepared.

DRINKS

There are 5 glasses of wine in a 750 ml (25 fl oz) bottle. For a two-hour wine and finger food party, allow 1 bottle between two people.

White wine is usually more popular than red so allow 1 bottle of red for every 2 white.

There are 6 glasses in a 750 ml (25 fl oz) bottle of Champagne. Allow 2½ glasses per person for a two-hour drinks party. Allow 1½ glasses per person as a drink before dinner.

Keep it simple. Serve drinks to fit your food 'theme', and not too many varieties.

Always supply soft drinks. For a two-hour drinks party, allow 1 glass per person. If only soft drinks are to be served and no alcohol, allow about 3 glasses per person.

* If people are bringing their own drinks, provide 1 glass per person in addition.

BEETROOT HUMMUS

80 ml ($^1/_3$ cup) olive oil
1 onion, chopped
450 g (16 oz) tin baby beetroot, drained
220 g (1 cup) ready-made hummus
2 garlic cloves, crushed
1 tablespoon ground cumin
1–2 tablespoons lemon juice

1 Heat 1 tablespoon oil in a frying pan, add the onion and cook for 3 minutes, or until soft but not brown.

2 Place the onion, beetroot, hummus, garlic, cumin and lemon juice in a food processor and process the mixture until it is smooth.

3 Transfer to a serving bowl, season with salt and pepper to taste and drizzle with the remaining olive oil.

INGREDIENTS

500 g (1 lb) orange sweet potato (kumera)
500 g (1 lb) beetroot
500 g (1 lb) parsnip
oil, for deep-frying

1   Preheat the oven to moderate 180°C (350°F/Gas 4).

2   Run a vegetable peeler along the length of the sweet potato and beetroot to make thin ribbons. Cut the parsnip into thin slices.

3   Fill a deep, heavy-based saucepan one-third full of oil and heat to 190°C (375°F), or until a cube of bread dropped into the oil browns in 10 seconds. Cook the vegetables in batches for about 30 seconds, or until golden and crisp, turning with tongs, if necessary. Drain on crumpled paper towels and season with salt. Keep warm on a baking tray in the oven and cook the remaining chips.

INGREDIENTS

155 g (1 1/4 cups) plain flour
pinch dry hot mustard
90 g (3 oz) butter, roughly chopped
60 g (1/2 cup) grated vintage Cheddar cheese
4 red chillies, seeded and sliced
1 egg yolk

1   Process the flour, mustard and butter until they resemble fine breadcrumbs. Add the cheese and chilli, then the egg yolk and 1 tablespoon water, and process until the mixture comes together. Gather into a ball, cover with plastic wrap and refrigerate for 30 minutes.

2   Preheat the oven to 190°C (375°F/Gas 5). On a lightly floured surface, roll out the dough to a 5 mm thickness. Cut into 5 cm rounds.

3   Place on lightly greased baking trays and bake for 15–20 minutes, or until golden. Cool.

135 g ($^1/_2$ cup) tahini
1 red chilli, seeded and finely chopped
$^1/_2$ teaspoon paprika
2 sheets ready-rolled puff pastry, thawed

1 Preheat the oven to 200°C (400°F/Gas 6). Combine the tahini, chilli and paprika.
Spread half the mixture over each sheet of pastry (to the edges).

2 Fold the pastry from opposite sides until the folds meet in the middle. Then fold one side
over the other to resemble a closed book. Refrigerate for 5 minutes to firm.

3 Cut into 1.5 cm ($^1/_2$ inch) slices and place on baking trays lined with baking paper
(leaving room for spreading).

4 Bake for 8 minutes, then turn over and bake for 2 minutes, or until golden brown.

TAHINI AND CHILLI PALMIERS

INGREDIENTS

1 red pepper (capsicum)
1 green pepper (capsicum)
1 yellow pepper (capsicum)
125 g (4 oz) cream cheese, softened
25 g ($^3/_4$ oz) Parmesan, grated
2 spring onions, finely chopped
$^1/_4$ cup (7 g/$^1/_4$ oz) chopped fresh oregano
1 tablespoon bottled capers, drained and chopped
1 tablespoon pine nuts, chopped
12 thin slices prosciutto

1 Cut the peppers into quarters and remove the seeds and membrane. Cook, skin-side-up, under a hot grill until the skin blackens and blisters. Place in a plastic bag until cool, then peel.

2 Mix together the cream cheese, Parmesan, spring onion, oregano, capers and pine nuts.

3 Place the pepper pieces on the prosciutto slices and trim the prosciutto to the same size. Remove the pepper and spread some cheese mixture on the prosciutto. Top with the pepper and spread with a little more cheese mixture. Roll up tightly from the short end. Cover and refrigerate for 1 hour, or until firm. Slice into 1 cm ($^1/_2$ inch) rounds and serve on toothpicks.

INGREDIENTS

16 large sardines
²/₃ cup (65 g/2¹/₄ oz) dry breadcrumbs
2 cloves garlic, crushed
2 tablespoons capers, drained and finely chopped
35 g (1¹/₄ oz) Parmesan, grated
2 egg yolks, lightly beaten
juice of 2 lemons, to serve

1 Preheat the oven to moderately hot 200°C (400°F/Gas 6). Lightly grease a baking tray.

2 Remove the heads from the sardines, make a slit through the gut and open out flat. Remove the guts and carefully scrape the flesh away from the backbone; trim at the tail end, leaving the tail intact. Lift out the backbone; discard. Wash the sardines well and drain on paper towels.

3 Mix together the breadcrumbs, garlic, capers, Parmesan, freshly ground black pepper and enough egg yolk to bind the stuffing together. Spoon a little onto each open sardine, put on the baking tray and bake for 20 minutes, or until golden. Serve warm or cold, drizzled with lemon juice.

NOTE You can buy sardines already filleted at some fishmongers. This makes the recipe quick and simple.

SUPPLI

3 cups (750 ml/24 fl oz) chicken stock
60 g (2 oz) butter
1 small onion, finely chopped
1²/₃ cups (360 g/12 oz) arborio rice
¹/₂ cup (125 ml/4 fl oz) white wine
pinch of powdered saffron
50 g (1³/₄ oz) Parmesan, grated
2 eggs, lightly beaten
100 g (3¹/₂ oz) mozzarella cheese
1 cup (100 g/3¹/₂ oz) dry breadcrumbs
oil, for deep-frying

1 Put the stock in a pan, bring to the boil, reduce the heat and maintain at simmering point. Heat the butter in a large heavy-based pan. Add the onion and cook for 2–3 minutes, until softened but not brown. Add the rice and stir for another 2–3 minutes, until well coated with butter and onion.

2 Add the combined wine and saffron and stir until all the wine is absorbed. Add ¹/₂ cup (125 ml/4 fl oz) stock to the rice and stir continuously until absorbed, then continue adding the stock a little at a time, stirring, until ¹/₂ cup stock remains (about 15 minutes). Add the remaining stock and stir, then cover with a tight-fitting lid. Reduce the heat to very low and cook for 10–15 minutes, until the rice is tender. Allow to cool.

3 Gently stir through the Parmesan, eggs and salt and pepper, to taste. Cut the mozzarella cheese into 30 small cubes. With wet hands, form the rice mixture into 30 walnut-sized balls. Push a cube of mozzarella into the centre of each ball and mould the rice around it.

4 Coat each ball with breadcrumbs. Chill for at least 1 hour to firm. Fill a deep heavy-based pan one third full of oil and heat the oil to 180°C (350°F). The oil is ready when a cube of bread turns golden brown in 15 seconds. Fry 3–4 balls at a time for 4–5 minutes, or until golden brown. Drain on crumpled paper towels. Serve hot.

NOTE The full name is Suppli al Telefono. Serve hot, so that when bitten into, the cheese filling pulls out into long thin strands like telephone wires.

INGREDIENTS

125 g (1 cup) plain (all-purpose) flour
$^1/_2$ teaspoon baking powder
$^1/_2$ teaspoon sugar
2 tablespoons linseeds
60 ml ($^1/_4$ cup) milk
2 tablespoons olive oil

1 Preheat the oven to 200°C (400°F/Gas 6). Process the flour, baking powder, sugar and $^1/_2$ teaspoon salt. Add pepper to taste, and stir in the linseeds. Add the milk and oil and mix to form a wet crumbly mixture, adding extra milk if the mixture is too dry.

2 Turn the mixture out onto a flat, lightly floured surface and bring the mixture together into a ball.

3 Divide the mixture in half, place one half between two sheets of baking paper and roll out to a thickness of 2–3 mm ($^1/_8$ inch). Prick liberally with a fork. Cut the dough into 12 irregular triangles and arrange in a single layer on a lightly greased baking tray. Repeat with the remaining dough.

4 Bake for 15–20 minutes, or until the bases are lightly golden. Turn over and bake for a further 4–5 minutes, or until the other side is also lightly golden. Transfer to a wire rack to cool completely.

FALAFEL

2 cups (440 g) dried chickpeas
1 onion, finely chopped
2 cloves garlic, crushed
2 tablespoons chopped fresh parsley
1 tablespoon chopped fresh coriander (cilantro)
2 teaspoons ground cumin
$^1/_2$ teaspoon baking powder
oil, for deep-frying

1 Soak the chickpeas in 3 cups (750 ml/24 fl oz) of water for 4 hours or overnight. Drain and place in a food processor, and process for 30 seconds, or until finely ground.

2 Add the onion, garlic, parsley, coriander, cumin, baking powder, 1 tablespoon of water, salt and pepper and process for 10 seconds, or until the mixture forms a rough paste. Cover and leave for 30 minutes.

3 Using your hands, shape heaped tablespoons of the falafel mixture into balls and squeeze out any excess liquid. Fill a deep heavy-based pan one-third full of oil to 180°C (350°F) and heat until a cube of bread browns in 15 seconds. Gently lower the falafel balls into the oil. Cook in batches of five at a time, for 3–4 minutes each batch. When the balls are browned, remove with a large slotted spoon. Drain well. Serve with Lebanese bread, tabbouleh and hummus.

INGREDIENTS

1 kg (2 lb) orange sweet potato (kumera)
1 tablespoon oil
30 g (1 oz) butter
4 leeks, white part only, finely sliced
2 cloves garlic, crushed
250 g (8 oz) feta cheese, crumbled
8 eggs
$^{1}/_{2}$ cup (125 ml/4 fl oz) cream

1   Preheat the oven to moderate 180°C (350°F/Gas 4). Grease or brush twelve 1 cup
    (250 ml/8 fl oz) muffin holes with oil or melted butter. Cut small rounds of baking paper
    and place into the base of each hole. Cut the sweet potato into small cubes and boil,
    steam or microwave until tender. Drain well and set aside.

2   Heat the oil and butter in a frying pan and cook the leek for 10 minutes, stirring
    occasionally, or until very soft and lightly golden. Add the garlic and cook for a further
    1 minute. Cool, then stir in the feta and sweet potato. Divide among the muffin holes.

3   Whisk the eggs and cream together and season with salt and cracked black pepper. Pour
    the egg mixture into each hole until three-quarters filled, then press the vegetables down
    gently. Bake for 25–30 minutes, or until golden and set. Leave in the tins for 5 minutes,
    then ease out with a knife. Delicious either served hot or at room temperature.

PESTO AND TOMATO TOASTS

Pesto
1 cup (50 g/1³/₄ oz) fresh basil leaves
¹/₂ cup (50 g/1³/₄ oz) pecan nuts
¹/₄ cup (60 ml/2 fl oz) olive oil
3 cloves garlic

1 French bread stick, thinly sliced
10 large sun-dried (sun-blushed) tomatoes, cut into thin
    strips
150 g (5 oz) Parmesan, thinly shaved

1 To make the pesto, mix the basil leaves, pecans, oil and garlic in a food processor until the mixture is smooth.

2 Toast the bread slices under a grill until brown on both sides.

3 Spread the pesto evenly over the pieces of toast. Top each slice with sun-dried tomatoes and some of the Parmesan.

2 cloves garlic, chopped
$1/2$ cup (125 ml/4 fl oz) olive oil
2 tablespoons finely chopped fresh dill
15 g ($1/2$ oz) finely chopped fresh parsley
2 tablespoons finely chopped fresh basil
2 tablespoons lemon juice
2 x 400 g (13 oz) cans artichoke hearts
3 tablespoons finely diced red capsicum (pepper)

1 To make the marinade, combine the garlic, oil, herbs and lemon juice in a bowl and whisk until well combined. Season with salt and cracked black pepper.

2 Drain the artichoke hearts and add to the marinade with the red pepper. Mix well to coat. Cover and marinate in the refrigerator overnight. Serve as part of an antipasto platter or use in salads. Return the artichokes to room temperature before serving.

GARLIC AND HERB MARINATED ARTICHOKES

CHICKEN TIKKA

$^1/_4$ onion, chopped

2 cloves garlic, crushed

1 tablespoon grated fresh ginger

2 tablespoons lemon juice

1 teaspoon grated lemon rind

3 teaspoons ground coriander (cilantro)

3 teaspoons ground cumin

3 teaspoons garam masala

$^1/_3$ cup (90 g/3 oz) plain yoghurt

1 teaspoon salt

750 g (1$^1/_2$ lb) chicken thigh fillets, cut into cubes

1 Soak 10 wooden skewers in water for 30 minutes to prevent burning.

2 In a food processor, finely chop the onion, garlic, ginger, lemon juice, rind, coriander, cumin and garam masala. Stir in the yoghurt and salt.

3 Thread 4–5 chicken cubes onto each skewer and place in a large shallow dish. Coat the skewers with the spice mixture. Marinate for several hours or overnight, covered, in the refrigerator.

4 Cook the skewers in batches on a barbecue or chargrill pan, or under a hot grill, for 3–4 minutes on each side, or until golden brown and cooked.

INGREDIENTS

Classic Tuscan
6 ripe Roma (plum) tomatoes
15 g ($^1/_2$ cup) basil, shredded
1 garlic clove, finely chopped
2 tablespoons extra virgin olive oil

Mushroom and parsley
2 tablespoons olive oil
200 g (7 oz) small button mushrooms, quartered
1 tablespoon lemon juice
50 g (1$^3/_4$ oz) goat's cheese, crumbled
1 tablespoon finely chopped flat-leaf (Italian) parsley
1 teaspoon chopped thyme

16 slices crusty white Italian-style bread, cut into 1 cm
  ($^1/_2$ inch) slices
4 garlic cloves, halved
60 ml ($^1/_4$ cup) olive oil

1 To make the classic Tuscan topping, score a cross in the base of each tomato and place in a bowl of boiling water for 10 seconds, then plunge into cold water. Peel the skin away from the cross. Cut in half and scoop out the seeds with a teaspoon. Finely dice the flesh, then combine with the basil, garlic and oil.

2 To make the mushroom and parsley topping, heat the oil in a frying pan and cook the mushrooms over medium heat for 5 minutes, or until just tender. Remove from the heat and transfer to a small bowl. Stir in the lemon juice, goat's cheese, parsley and thyme.

3 Toast the bread and, while still hot, rub with the cut side of a garlic clove. Drizzle oil over each slice of bread, then season with salt and freshly ground black pepper. Divide the toppings among the bread slices.

NOTE Each topping makes enough for eight slices of bruschetta. You will only need eight slices of bread if you only want to make one topping.

CRUNCHY WEDGES

6 floury or all-purpose potatoes

1 tablespoon oil

25 g ($^1/_4$ cup) dry breadcrumbs

2 teaspoons chopped chives

1 teaspoon celery salt

$^1/_4$ teaspoon garlic powder

$^1/_2$ teaspoon chopped rosemary

1 Preheat the oven to 200°C (400°F/Gas 6). Cut the potatoes into eight wedges each and toss in the oil.

2 Combine the breadcrumbs, chives, celery salt, garlic powder and rosemary in a bowl. Add the wedges and coat well. Place on greased baking trays and bake for 40 minutes, or until crisp and golden.

20 cherry bocconcini or ovolini, or 5 regular bocconcini, sliced into quarters
2 tablespoons olive oil
2 tablespoons chopped fresh parsley
1 tablespoon chopped fresh chives
20 small cherry tomatoes
40 small fresh basil leaves

1   Put the bocconcini in a bowl with the oil, parsley, chives, $1/4$ teaspoon salt and $1/2$ teaspoon ground black pepper. Cover and refrigerate for at least 1 hour, or preferably overnight.

2   Cut each cherry tomato in half and thread one half on a skewer or toothpick, followed by a basil leaf, then bocconcini, another basil leaf and then another tomato half. Repeat with more skewers and the remaining ingredients and serve.

BOCCONCINO TOMATO SKEWERS

PUMPKIN AND PESTO CHICKEN IN FILO PASTRY

4 chicken breast fillets
1 tablespoon oil
250 g (8 oz) pumpkin
1 bunch English spinach
12 sheets filo pastry
100 g (3$^{1}/_{2}$ oz) butter, melted
$^{1}/_{4}$ cup (25 g/$^{3}/_{4}$ oz) dry breadcrumbs
100 g (3$^{1}/_{2}$ oz) ricotta
$^{1}/_{3}$ cup (90 g/3 oz) pesto
1 tablespoon pine nuts, chopped

1 Preheat the oven to moderately hot 200°C (400°F/Gas 6). Season the chicken fillets with salt and pepper. Heat half the oil in a frying pan and fry the chicken until browned on both sides, then remove from the pan.

2 Cut the peeled pumpkin into 5 mm (¼ inch) slices. Heat the remaining oil in the same pan and fry the pumpkin until lightly browned on both sides. Allow to cool.

3 Put the spinach leaves into a bowl of boiling water and stir until just wilted. Drain well and pat dry with paper towels. Layer 3 sheets of filo pastry, brushing each with some of the melted butter, sprinkling between layers with some of the breadcrumbs.

4 Wrap each chicken breast in a quarter of the spinach and place on one short side of the filo, leaving a 2 cm (¾ inch) gap. Top the chicken with a quarter of the pumpkin slices, then spread a quarter of the ricotta down the centre of the pumpkin. Top with a table-spoon of the pesto.

5 Fold the sides of the pastry over the filling, then roll the parcel up until it sits on the unsecured end. Repeat with the remaining ingredients. Place the parcels on a lightly greased baking tray, brush with any remaining butter and sprinkle with the pine nuts. Bake for 15 minutes, then cover loosely with foil and bake for a further 20 minutes, or until the pastry is golden brown.

INGREDIENTS

500 g (1 lb) mixed nuts (almonds, brazil nuts, pecans, macadamias, cashew nuts)
1 egg white
2 tablespoons curry powder
1 teaspoon ground cumin

1 Preheat the oven to slow 150°C (300°F/Gas 2). Spread the nuts in a single layer on a baking tray and roast for 10 minutes.

2 Whisk the egg white until frothy, then add the nuts, curry powder, cumin and 1 teaspoon salt. Toss together and return to the oven for a further 10–15 minutes, then allow to cool.

THAI CHICKEN MEATBALLS

1 kg (2 lb) chicken mince
1 cup (80 g/2³/₄ oz) fresh breadcrumbs
4 spring onions, sliced
1 tablespoon ground coriander (cilantro)
1 cup (50 g/1³/₄ oz) chopped coriander (cilantro)
¹/₄ cup (60 ml/2 fl oz) sweet chilli sauce
1–2 tablespoons lemon juice
oil, for frying

1 Preheat the oven to moderately hot 200°C (400°F/Gas 6). Mix the mince and bread-crumbs in a large bowl.

2 Add the spring onion, ground and fresh coriander, chilli sauce and lemon juice, and mix well. Using damp hands, form the mixture into evenly shaped balls that are either small enough to eat with your fingers or large enough to use as burgers.

3 Heat the oil in a deep frying pan, and shallow-fry the chicken balls in batches over high heat until browned all over. Place the chicken balls on a baking tray and bake until cooked through. (The small chicken balls will take 5 minutes to cook and the larger ones will take 10–15 minutes.) This mixture also makes a delicious filling for sausage rolls.

INGREDIENTS

250 g (8 oz) cream cheese or neufchatel
210 g (7 oz) can red or pink salmon, drained
1 tablespoon sour cream
1 tablespoon mayonnaise
1–2 teaspoons lemon juice
1 tablespoon finely chopped fresh coriander (cilantro)
1 tablespoon finely chopped fresh chives
2 teaspoons finely chopped fresh lemon thyme
4 Lebanese cucumbers, thickly sliced
sprigs of fresh dill or thinly shredded chilli or red pepper (capsicum), to decorate

1   Beat the cream cheese in a small bowl with electric beaters until soft and creamy. Add the salmon, sour cream, mayonnaise, lemon juice, coriander, chives, lemon thyme, and salt and pepper. Beat for 1 minute, or until combined.

2   Place a teaspoon of the cheese mixture on each cucumber round and decorate.

INGREDIENTS

1¹/₂ cups (185 g/6 oz) plain (all-purpose) flour
100 g (3¹/₂ oz) chilled butter, chopped
30 g (1 oz) Parmesan, grated
1 egg, lightly beaten

Fillings

pesto, sun-dried (sun-blushed) tomato and black olives

olive tapenade, hard-boiled quail eggs and fresh flat-leaf parsley

cream cheese, shredded sliced smoked salmon, thinly sliced Lebanese cucumber, and chopped fresh chives

1 Sift the flour and ¹/₄ teaspoon salt into a large bowl, add the butter and rub into the flour with your fingertips until the mixture resembles fine breadcrumbs. Stir in the Parmesan, then make a well in the centre. Add the egg and a little water and mix with a flat-bladed knife, using a cutting action, until the mixture comes together in beads. Gently gather together and lift out onto a lightly floured surface. Press together into a ball. Wrap in plastic wrap and refrigerate for 30 minutes.

2 Preheat the oven to hot 210°C (415°F/Gas 6–7). Lightly grease two 12-hole round-based patty tins. Roll the pastry out very thinly and using an 8 cm (3 inch) cutter, cut 30 rounds from the pastry. Press the pastry into the tins and prick lightly all over. Bake for 8–9 minutes, or until golden. Allow to cool in the tins. Remove and repeat with the remaining pastry.

3 Fill the cooled shells with the different fillings.

INGREDIENTS

225 g (7 oz) feta cheese, crumbled
200 g (6¹/₂ oz) cream cheese, slightly softened
2 eggs, lightly beaten
¹/₄ teaspoon ground nutmeg
20 sheets filo pastry
60 g (2 oz) butter, melted
3 tablespoons sesame seeds

1   Preheat the oven to moderate 180°C (350°F/Gas 4). Place the feta, cream cheese, egg and nutmeg in a bowl and mix until just combined—the mixture will be lumpy.

2   Work with five sheets of pastry at a time, keeping the rest covered with a damp tea towel. Lay each sheet on a work surface, brush with melted butter and lay them on top of each other. Use a ruler as guidance to cut the filo into six equal strips.

3   Place 1 tablespoon of the filling at one end of a strip, leaving a narrow border. Fold the pastry over to enclose the filling and form a triangle. Continue folding the triangle over until you reach the end of the pastry, tucking any excess pastry under. Repeat with the remaining ingredients to make 24 triangles, and place on a lined baking tray.

4   Lightly brush with the remaining melted butter and sprinkle with sesame seeds. Bake for 15–20 minutes, or until puffed and golden.

CHEESE AND SPINACH ROULADE BRUSCHETTA

INGREDIENTS

1 French bread stick
2 tablespoons oil
500 g (1 lb) English spinach
90 g (3 oz) spreadable cream cheese
90 g (3 oz) goats cheese
3 tablespoons canned pimiento, drained and finely chopped

1 Preheat the oven to moderately hot 200°C (400°F/Gas 6). Cut the bread into 24 thin slices and lightly brush both sides with oil. Bake in a single layer on a baking tray for 10 minutes, or until lightly browned, turning once. Remove and allow to cool.

2 Remove the stalks from the spinach and place the leaves in a bowl. Cover with boiling water and leave for a couple of minutes, or until the leaves have wilted. Drain and leave to cool. Squeeze out the excess liquid and drain on crumpled paper towels.

3 Lay the spinach leaves flat, overlapping, on a piece of plastic wrap, to form a 25 x 20 cm (10 x 8 inch) rectangle. Beat the cheeses together until soft and smooth. Spread the cheese mixture evenly and carefully over the spinach. Top the cheese evenly with pimiento. Using the plastic wrap as a guide, carefully roll up the spinach to enclose the cheese. Remove the plastic wrap and cut the log into thin slices using a sharp knife. Serve on the toast.

NOTE Be sure to thoroughly drain the spinach and pimiento to avoid a watery result.

INGREDIENTS

1 kg (2 lb) English spinach
¹/₄ cup (60 ml/2 fl oz) olive oil
1 onion, chopped
10 spring onions, sliced
¹/₃ cup (20 g/³/₄ oz) chopped fresh parsley
1 tablespoon chopped fresh dill
large pinch of ground nutmeg
¹/₃ cup (35 g/1¹/₄ oz) freshly grated Parmesan
150 g (5 oz) crumbled feta cheese
90 g (3 oz) ricotta cheese
4 eggs, lightly beaten
40 g (1¹/₄ oz) butter, melted
1 tablespoon olive oil, extra
12 sheets filo pastry

1   Trim any coarse stems from the spinach. Wash the leaves thoroughly, roughly chop and place in a large pan with just a little water clinging to the leaves. Cover and cook gently over low heat for 5 minutes, or until the leaves have wilted. Drain well and allow to cool slightly before squeezing tightly to remove the excess water.

2   Heat the oil in a heavy-based frying pan. Add the onion and cook over low heat for 10 minutes, or until tender and golden. Add the spring onion and cook for a further 3 minutes. Remove from the heat. Stir in the drained spinach, parsley, dill, nutmeg, Parmesan, feta, ricotta and egg. Season well.

3   Preheat the oven to moderate 180°C (350°F/Gas 4). Grease two baking trays. Combine the melted butter with the extra oil. Work with three sheets of pastry at a time, keeping the rest covered with a damp tea towel. Brush each sheet with butter mixture and lay them on top of each other. Cut in half lengthways.

4   Spoon 4 tablespoons of the filling on an angle at the end of each strip. Fold the pastry over to enclose the filling and form a triangle. Continue folding the triangle over until your reach the end of the pastry. Put the triangles on the baking trays and brush with the remaining butter mixture. Bake for 20–25 minutes, or until the pastry is golden brown.

NOTE   Feta is a salty Greek cheese that should be stored immersed in lightly salted water in the fridge. Rinse and pat dry before using.

SPINACH AND FETA TRIANGLES

INGREDIENTS

Basil pesto
25 g ($^3/_4$ oz) fresh basil leaves
30 g (1 oz) Parmesan, grated
2 tablespoons pine nuts, toasted
2 tablespoons olive oil

1 small clove garlic, crushed
2$^1/_2$ tablespoons olive oil
1 sourdough bread stick, cut into 24 x 1 cm ($^1/_2$ inch) thick
  slices
500 g (1 lb) small flat mushrooms, thinly sliced
3 teaspoons balsamic vinegar
80 g (2$^3/_4$ oz) thinly sliced prosciutto

1   For the basil pesto, finely chop the basil leaves, Parmesan and pine nuts in a food
    processor. Gradually add the olive oil in a thin stream, with the motor running, and process
    until smooth. Season with salt and pepper.

2   Combine the garlic with 2 tablespoons of the olive oil in a small bowl and brush it over
    both sides of the bread slices. Place on baking trays and cook both sides under a
    medium-hot grill until golden brown.

3   Heat the remaining $^1/_2$ tablespoon of olive oil in a large frying pan. Add the mushrooms
    and cook over medium heat for 3–4 minutes, or until the mushrooms are heated through.
    Drain away any liquid. Add the pesto and the vinegar to the mushrooms, stir to combine,
    then cook over low heat for 1–2 minutes, or until heated through.

4   Preheat the oven to moderately hot 200°C (400°F/Gas 6). To assemble, top the toasts
    with mushroom, then torn and folded prosciutto. Bake on baking trays for 6 minutes, or
    until the prosciutto is crisp. Serve immediately.

INGREDIENTS

2 cups (250 g/8 oz) plain (all-purpose) flour
3 teaspoons baking powder
110 g (3¹/₂ oz) chilled butter
100 g (3¹/₂ oz) Stilton cheese
2 tablespoons chopped fresh chives
³/₄ cup (185 ml/6 fl oz) milk

Filling

1 cup (250 ml/8 fl oz) port
6 large dried figs, stems removed
1 teaspoon sugar
1 large leek
1 teaspoon Dijon mustard
2 teaspoons red wine vinegar
1 tablespoon olive oil
150 g (5 oz) shaved ham

1 Sift the flour, baking powder and ³/₄ teaspoon salt into a large bowl. Coarsely grate the butter and cheese into the flour and rub in with your fingertips until the pieces are the size of coarse breadcrumbs. Stir in the chives. Pour in the milk and combine with a fork until large clumps form. Turn onto a floured surface and press into a ball.

2 On a floured surface, roll the dough into a 15 x 25 cm (6 x 10 inch) rectangle. With the long edge of the dough facing you, fold in both ends so they meet in the centre, then fold the dough in half widthways. Roll again into a 15 x 25 cm (6 x 10 inch) rectangle, about 1 cm (1/2 inch) thick. Cut rounds close together with a 3 cm (1¹/₄ inch) cutter. Push the scraps together and roll and cut as before. Place 2.5 cm (1 inch) apart on a baking tray and refrigerate for 20 minutes. Preheat the oven to hot 220°C (425°F/Gas 7) and bake for 10–12 minutes, or until lightly browned.

3 In a small pan, heat the port, figs and sugar. Bring to the boil, reduce the heat and simmer for 15 minutes. Remove the figs and, when cooled, roughly chop. Simmer the liquid for about 3 minutes, until reduced and syrupy. Put the figs back in and stir to combine. Set aside.

4 Discard any tough leaves from the leek, then rinse the leek. Trim off the dark green tops. Slit the leek lengthways, almost to the bottom, roll a quarter turn and slit again. Wash well, drain and steam for about 10 minutes, or until very soft. Roughly chop, then combine with the mustard, vinegar and oil. Season with salt and pepper.

5 Cut the scones in half. Put a folded piece of ham on each bottom half, top with a teaspoon each of leek and fig mixture, then replace the tops.

INGREDIENTS

500 g (1 lb) piece beef eye fillet, trimmed
2 teaspoons oil
60 g (2 oz) butter, melted
1 clove garlic, crushed
2 small bread sticks, cut into very thin slices
25 g (³/₄ oz) mustard cress, cut in short lengths

Béarnaise
200 g (6¹/₂ oz) butter, melted
¹/₃ cup (80 ml/2³/₄ fl oz) white wine vinegar
1 bay leaf
1 tablespoon chopped fresh tarragon
6 black peppercorns
3 fresh parsley stalks
2 egg yolks
2 teaspoons chopped fresh tarragon, extra

1 Preheat the oven to moderate 180°C (350°F/Gas 4). Tie the beef with string at even intervals; season. Heat the oil in a pan and fry the beef to brown all over. Transfer to a small baking dish and bake for 20–25 minutes for medium to medium-rare. Remove and set aside.

2 Combine the butter and garlic in a bowl and brush over both sides of the bread. Bake on baking trays for 10 minutes, or until just golden.

3 For the Béarnaise, melt the butter slowly over low heat, remove from the heat and leave for 2–3 minutes to allow the milky mixture to separate to the bottom. Pour off the butter, leaving the milky sediment behind; discard the sediment. Combine the vinegar, bay leaf, tarragon, peppercorns and parsley in a pan and simmer briefly until reduced to 1 table-spoon; strain. Beat the egg yolks and the reduced sauce in a heatproof bowl over a pan of simmering water until slightly thickened. Remove from the heat and drizzle in the butter a few drops at a time, beating continuously until thick. Stir in the extra tarragon and season, to taste. If the mixture becomes too thick (it should be the consistency of mayonnaise), stir in a little water. If the butter is added too quickly, the mixture will separate.

4 Cut the beef into very thin slices, drape on each crouton and top with Béarnaise. Place the mustard cress on the Béarnaise.

INGREDIENTS

Filling
300 g (10 oz) ocean trout fillet
$\frac{1}{4}$ cup (60 ml/2 fl oz) lemon juice
2 tablespoons extra virgin olive oil
$\frac{1}{2}$ small Lebanese cucumber, finely chopped
2 spring onions, finely sliced
1 tablespoon chopped fresh dill or chervil
20 baby English spinach leaves

1 cup (125 g/4 oz) plain (all-purpose) flour
2 tablespoons grated Parmesan
75 g (2$\frac{1}{2}$ oz) chilled butter, cubed
1 egg, lightly beaten

1   Remove the skin from the trout, then, using kitchen tweezers, remove the bones. Freeze the fish in plastic wrap for 1 hour. Whisk the lemon juice and oil in a bowl. Cut the fish into strips about 3 x 1 cm (1$\frac{1}{4}$ x $\frac{1}{2}$ inch) and add to the lemon juice marinade. Cover and set aside at room temperature for 20 minutes, or until the fish turns opaque (in summer, refrigerate—the process will take a little longer). Drain off most of the marinade, leaving just enough to moisten the fish. Add the cucumber, spring onion, dill or chervil, and season with salt and black pepper.

2   While the fish is marinating, sift the flour and a pinch of salt into a large bowl and add the Parmesan and butter. Rub in with your fingertips until the mixture resembles fine breadcrumbs. Make a well, add the egg and stir in with a flat-bladed knife until the mixture comes together in beads. Turn onto a lightly floured surface and gather into a ball. Wrap in plastic wrap and refrigerate for 30 minutes.

3   Preheat the oven to hot 210°C (415°F/Gas 6–7). Lightly grease two 12-hole round-based patty tins. Roll out the pastry to about 2 mm ($\frac{1}{8}$ inch) thick and cut 8 cm (3 inch) rounds to line 20 holes. Prick the pastry lightly with a fork and bake for 8–10 minutes, or until golden. Remove from the tins and set aside to cool. Place a spinach leaf in each tart case and top with 1 level tablespoon of filling. Serve at once.

INGREDIENTS

500 g (1 lb) minced (ground) lamb
1 small onion, finely chopped
1 clove garlic, crushed
1 teaspoon ground coriander (cilantro)
1 teaspoon ground cumin
$1/4$ teaspoon ground cinnamon
$1/2$ teaspoon finely chopped red chilli
1 teaspoon tomato paste (tomato purée)
1 tablespoon chopped fresh mint
1 tablespoon chopped fresh coriander (cilantro)
oil, for frying

Yoghurt dip
1 small tomato, peeled, seeded and finely chopped
$1/2$ Lebanese cucumber, peeled and finely chopped
1 clove garlic, crushed
1 tablespoon chopped fresh mint
$1/2$ cup (125 g/4 oz) natural yoghurt

1 Combine the mince, onion, garlic, coriander, cumin, cinnamon, chilli, tomato paste and mint and coriander leaves in a large bowl and mix well with your hands. Season well, then roll into small balls (about $1 1/2$ teaspoons each).

2 Place a large heavy-based frying pan over moderate heat and heat a little oil. Cook the koftas in batches until well browned all over and cooked through. Drain on crumpled paper towels.

3 Mix together the dip ingredients and place in a small bowl.

4 Skewer each kofta with a cocktail stick and serve with the dip.

INGREDIENTS

1 tablespoon oil
1 clove garlic, crushed
1 tablespoon grated fresh ginger
1 tablespoon finely chopped lemon grass, white part only
1 onion, finely chopped
1 tablespoon tandoori curry paste
4 kaffir lime (makrut) leaves, finely shredded
1 tablespoon coconut cream
2 teaspoons grated lime rind
600 g (1¼ lb) raw prawns (shrimp), peeled and deveined
12 stems lemon grass, cut into 15 cm (6 inch) lengths, halved lengthways

1   Heat the oil in a frying pan, add the garlic, ginger, lemon grass and onion and stir over
    medium heat for 3 minutes, or until golden.

2   Add the tandoori paste and kaffir lime leaves to the pan and cook for 5 minutes, or until
    the tandoori paste is fragrant. Allow to cool slightly. Transfer to a food processor, add the
    coconut cream, lime rind and prawns and mix until finely minced. Divide into 24 portions
    and, with wet hands, shape one portion around each piece of lemon grass stem,
    leaving about 3 cm (1¼ inches) uncovered at each end. The mixture is quite soft,
    so take care when handling it. Using wet hands makes the mixture easier to manage.
    Refrigerate for 1 hour.

3   Grill the satays under a medium heat for 5 minutes, or until cooked through.

INGREDIENTS

20 large cooked prawns (shrimp)
100 g (3¹/₂ oz) dried mung bean vermicelli (cellophane
    noodles)
20–25 rice paper wrappers, about 16 cm (6¹/₂ inches) round
40 fresh mint leaves
10 garlic chives, cut in halves

Dipping sauce
2 tablespoons satay sauce
3 tablespoons hoisin sauce
1 red chilli, finely chopped
1 tablespoon chopped roasted unsalted peanuts
1 tablespoon lemon juice

1 Peel the prawns and gently pull out the dark vein from the backs, starting at the head end. Cut all the prawns in half.

2 Soak the vermicelli for 5 minutes in a bowl with enough hot water to cover. Drain well and use scissors to roughly chop the noodles into shorter lengths.

3 Working with one rice paper wrapper at a time, dip into a bowl of warm water, leave for about 30 seconds, or until the wrapper becomes soft and pliable, then remove. Be careful as the wrappers can tear easily when softened.

4 Place 1 softened wrapper on a work surface and spoon about 1 tablespoon of the noodles along the bottom third of the wrapper, leaving enough space at the sides to fold the wrapper over. Top with 2 mint leaves and 2 prawn halves. Fold in the sides towards each other and firmly roll up the wrapper, adding the piece of garlic chive as you roll so it points out of one side. Repeat with the remaining wrappers and ingredients and place the spring rolls, seam-side-down, on a serving plate.

5 For the dipping sauce, mix the ingredients in a small bowl. Serve with the spring rolls.

INGREDIENTS

400 g (13 oz) rice vermicelli
oil, for shallow-frying
2 teaspoons sesame oil
2 carrots, cut into matchsticks
1 red capsicum (pepper), cut into matchsticks
2 zucchini (courgettes), cut into julienne strips
4 spring onions, cut into julienne strips
$1/2$–1 tablespoon oyster sauce

1 Soak the vermicelli for 3 minutes in a bowl with enough boiling water to cover, then drain thoroughly until very dry.

2 Heat the oil in a large heavy-based frying pan over medium heat. Shape tablespoons of the noodles into flat discs and shallow-fry in batches for 3 minutes, or until crisp and golden. Drain on crumpled paper towels.

3 Heat the sesame oil in a wok and stir-fry the vegetables for 3 minutes until softened slightly. Stir in the oyster sauce and cook for 2 minutes. Serve the cakes topped with the vegetables.

INGREDIENTS

1 cup (125 g) plain (all-purpose) flour
2 tablespoons self-raising flour
1 teaspoon curry powder
125 g butter
$^1/_2$ cup (50 g) grated Parmesan
$^2/_3$ cup (85 g) grated Cheddar
20 g crumbled blue-vein cheese
1 tablespoon lemon juice
$^1/_4$ cup (25 g) finely grated Parmesan, extra

1   Place the flours, curry powder and butter in a food processor. Process until the mixture resembles fine breadcrumbs.

2   Stir in the cheeses and the lemon juice. Bring the mixture together into a ball.

3   Roll into a 30 cm (12 inch) log. Wrap in plastic wrap and chill for 1 hour. Slice into 5 mm ($^1/_4$ inch) slices. Reshape if necessary. Preheat the oven to moderately hot 200°C (400°F/Gas 6).

4   Place on a baking paper-lined oven tray, allowing some room for spreading. Sprinkle the tops with Parmesan. Bake for 15 minutes, or until the biscuits are golden. Cool on the trays.

INGREDIENTS

1 tablespoon oil
2 cloves garlic, crushed
1 tablespoon grated fresh ginger
2 spring onions, chopped
500 g (1 lb) raw prawns (shrimp), peeled and chopped
$^1/_2$ teaspoon fish sauce
$^1/_2$ teaspoon sugar
1 tablespoon lemon juice
2 tablespoons chopped fresh coriander (cilantro)
6 large spring roll wrappers, cut into quarters
oil, for deep-frying
fresh chives, for serving
sweet chilli sauce, for serving

1   Heat the oil in a frying pan, add the garlic and ginger and cook over low heat for 2
    minutes. Add the spring onion and cook for 2 minutes. Increase the heat to high, add the
    prawns and stir-fry for 2 minutes, or until the colour just changes. Be careful not to
    overcook the prawns or they will become tough once deep-fried.

2   Add the fish sauce, sugar, lemon juice and coriander to the pan. Toss with the prawns for
    1 minute. Remove from the heat; cool slightly.

3   Divide the cooled mixture into 24 portions. Place one portion in the centre of each piece
    of spring roll wrapper. Brush the edges with water and fold to form a parcel.

4   Fill a deep heavy-based pan one third full of oil. Heat the oil to 180°C (350°F). The oil is
    hot enough when a cube of bread dropped into the oil turns golden brown in 15 seconds.
    Deep-fry the parcels one at a time, holding them with tongs for the first few seconds to
    keep them intact. Cook until golden brown. Drain on crumpled paper towels. Tie with
    lengths of chives. Serve with sweet chilli sauce.

NOTE If the spring roll wrappers are very thin, you may need to use two together.

INGREDIENTS

7 g sachet dried yeast
pinch of sugar
1 cup (250 ml) warm milk
$^3/_4$ cup (100 g) buckwheat flour
$^1/_2$ cup (60 g) plain (all-purpose) flour
2 eggs, separated
20 g butter
$^1/_3$ cup (80 ml) oil
150 g crème fraîche
300 g (10$^1/_2$ oz) smoked salmon, cut into 2 cm (1 inch) strips
50 g (1$^3/_4$ oz) salmon roe
fresh dill sprigs, to garnish

1   Place the yeast and sugar in a small bowl and gradually stir in the milk. Sift the flours into a large bowl and make a well in the centre. Add the egg yolks and warm milk mixture and whisk until combined and smooth. Cover and stand in a warm place for 45 minutes to prove.

2   Melt the butter, then stir into the proved dough and season. Place the egg whites in a clean dry bowl and beat with electric beaters until soft peaks form. Fold one third of the egg whites into the batter until just mixed. Gently fold in the remaining egg whites until just combined.

3   Heat 1 tablespoon of the oil in a large frying pan over medium heat. Drop $^1/_2$ tablespoon of batter into the pan for each blini. Cook for 1 minute, or until bubbles form on the surface. Turn over and cook for 30 seconds, or until golden. Repeat to make about 40 blini, adding more oil as needed. Cool completely.

4   Spread 1 teaspoon of crème fraîche on each blini, then arrange a strip of smoked salmon over it. Spoon $^1/_4$ teaspoon of salmon roe on top. Garnish with a sprig of dill and serve.

INGREDIENTS

4 Lebanese cucumbers
oil, for pan-frying
250 g fillet steak
$1/2$ red onion, finely chopped
20 fresh mint leaves, finely chopped
1 tablespoon finely chopped fresh coriander (cilantro) leaves
$1^1/_2$ tablespoons fish sauce
$1^1/_2$ tablespoons lime juice
1 bird's eye chilli, seeded and finely chopped
1 teaspoon grated palm sugar or soft brown sugar
small coriander (cilantro) leaves, to garnish

1 Trim each end of the cucumbers but do not peel them. Cut each cucumber into 2 cm (1 inch) thick slices; you should get 24 pieces. Scoop out the centre of each slice with a melon baller, leaving a shell of flesh.

2 Heat a large frying pan over high heat and brush lightly with oil. Season beef with salt and pepper, then place in pan and cook for $1^1/_2$–2 minutes each side, depending on the thickness (the beef needs to be rare). Set aside to rest for 5 minutes. Thinly slice beef across the grain, then slice each piece into 5 mm ($^1/_4$ inch) wide strips and transfer to a bowl.

3 Add the onion, mint and coriander to the bowl and mix well. Combine the fish sauce, lime juice, chilli and sugar, stirring until the sugar has dissolved. Pour over the beef mixture and mix well. Fill each cucumber cup with the Thai beef salad and garnish with a whole coriander leaf.

CUCUMBER CUPS WITH THAI BEEF SALAD

PORK SAN CHOY BAU

1 tablespoon oil

400 g (13 oz) minced (ground) pork

230 g (7¹/₂ oz) can water chestnuts, drained and chopped finely

125 g (4 oz) canned bamboo shoots, drained and chopped finely

6 spring onions, finely chopped

2 tablespoons dry sherry

1 tablespoon soy sauce

2 teaspoons sesame oil

2 teaspoons oyster sauce

tiny lettuce leaves (cos, iceberg or witlof)

chopped fresh mint, for serving

Sauce

2 tablespoons plum sauce

1 tablepoon hoisin sauce

1 teaspoon soy sauce

1 Heat the oil in a pan or wok, add the pork and cook, stirring, over high heat until brown all over. Break up any lumps of mince with the back of a fork. Add the water chestnuts, bamboo shoots and spring onion, toss well and cook for 1 minute.

2 Combine the sherry, soy sauce, sesame oil and oyster sauce, add to the wok, toss well and cook for 2 minutes. Remove from the heat.

3 To make the dipping sauce, stir all the ingredients in a bowl with 2 tablespoons water.

4 To serve, put about 1 tablespoon of warm pork mixture on each lettuce leaf. Sprinkle with the chopped mint. Serve with the sauce, for drizzling over the top.

INGREDIENTS

20 rice paper wrappers
350 g (11 oz) raw prawn (shrimp) meat
4 cm (1½ inch) piece fresh ginger, grated
2 cloves garlic, crushed
3 spring onions, finely chopped
1 tablespoon rice flour
1 egg white, beaten
2 teaspoons sesame oil
2 tablespoons cornflour (cornstarch)
oil, for deep frying
2 tablespoons sesame seeds, toasted
plum sauce, for serving, optional

1 Place 4 rice paper wrappers on a work surface. Brush generously with water, then leave for 2 minutes, or until soft and pliable. Gently transfer to a plate (they may be stacked on top of each other at this stage). Repeat the brushing with the remaining wrappers, then cover with plastic wrap.

2 Finely chop the prawn meat and combine with the ginger, garlic, spring onion, rice flour, egg white, sesame oil and some salt and pepper. Mix very well with your fingertips. Blend the cornflour with 2 tablespoons water in a small bowl. Working with one wrapper at a time, spread one tablespoon of prawn mixture across the wrapper, just below the centre. Fold up the bottom section to encase the filling. Roll the wrapper over once, lightly pushing down to flatten out the filling. Fold in the sides and brush the edges with cornflour mixture, then wrap to form a parcel. Put on double thickness paper towels and repeat with the remaining wrappers and filling.

3 Fill a deep heavy-based pan one third full of oil and heat to 180°C (350°F). The oil is ready when a cube of bread dropped into the oil turns golden brown in 15 seconds. Add several parcels and cook for 4–5 minutes, or until golden brown. Remove with a slotted spoon or tongs, drain on crumpled paper towels and repeat with the remainder. Sprinkle with sesame seeds. Serve with plum sauce, if desired.

NOTE Rice paper wrappers are available in some speciality shops and Asian supermarkets.

INGREDIENTS

2 cups (250 g/9 oz) plain flour
125 g chilled butter, chopped
1 egg

Filling
300 g (10½ oz) cherry tomatoes, quartered
2 tablespoons olive oil
1 clove garlic, crushed
200 g (7 oz) bocconcini, quartered
80 g (3 oz) chopped Kalamata olives
1 tablespoon extra virgin olive oil
1 tablespoon torn fresh basil
oil, for deep-frying
30 small fresh basil leaves

1   Preheat the oven to moderately hot 200°C (400°F/Gas 6). Grease 30 mini muffin holes. Sift the flour and rub the butter in with your fingertips until the mixture resembles fine breadcrumbs. Make a well, add the egg and mix with a flat-bladed knife, using a cutting action, until it gathers in beads. Add a little cold water if necessary. Press the dough into a ball, wrap in plastic wrap and chill for 30 minutes.

2   Roll out the dough between two sheets of baking paper to 2 mm (⅛ inch) thick and cut 30 rounds with a 6 cm (2 inch) cutter. Press a round into each muffin hole. Prick each base with a fork and bake for 6 minutes, or until dry and golden. If they puff up, use a clean tea towel to press back. Cool.

3   To make the filling, preheat the oven to moderately hot 200°C (400°F/Gas 6). Combine the tomatoes, olive oil and garlic in a roasting tin and bake for 15 minutes, or until golden. Cool, add the bocconcini, olives, extra virgin olive oil and basil, season, and toss. Fill a saucepan one-third full of oil and heat to 180°C (350°F), or until a cube of bread browns in 15 seconds. Deep-fry the basil in batches for 30 seconds, or until crisp. Drain. Spoon the vegetable mixture into the pastry cases and top with a basil leaf.

INGREDIENTS

500 g (1 lb) firm white fish fillets
4 kaffir lime (makrut) leaves, finely shredded
1 tablespoon chopped fresh Asian basil
2 tablespoons red curry paste
100 g (3¹/₂ oz) green beans, very finely sliced
2 spring onions, finely chopped
oil, for shallow-frying

Cucumber dipping sauce

1 Lebanese cucumber, finely chopped
3 tablespoons sweet chilli sauce
2 tablespoons rice vinegar
1 tablespoon chopped unsalted roasted peanuts
1 tablespoon chopped fresh coriander (cilantro)

1 Briefly chop the fish in a food processor until smooth. Add the lime leaves, basil and curry paste and process for 10 seconds. Transfer to a large bowl, add the beans and spring onion and mix well. Wet your hands and form level tablespoons of the mixture into small, flattish patties.

2 Mix all the sauce ingredients in a bowl.

3 Heat the oil in a heavy-based frying pan over medium heat. Cook the fish cakes, in batches, until golden brown on both sides. Drain on paper towels and serve with the dipping sauce.

THAI FISH CAKES

INGREDIENTS

24 fresh oysters (see note)
1 tablespoon chopped fresh dill
1 clove garlic, crushed
1 tablespoon finely chopped fresh flat-leaf parsley
2 teaspoons finely chopped fresh chives
2 tablespoons lemon juice
1/4 cup (60 ml) extra virgin olive oil
chive bows, to garnish
brown (wholemeal) bread, cubed, to garnish

1 Remove the oysters from the shells and pat dry. Wash the shells, replace the oysters and cover with a damp cloth in the fridge.

2 Place the dill, garlic, parsley, chives, lemon juice and oil in a bowl and season to taste with salt and cracked black pepper. Mix together well, then drizzle a little of the dressing over each oyster.

3 Garnish with chive bows and serve with tiny cubes of brown bread.

NOTE Oysters are sold freshly shucked on the half shell, or alive and unshucked. When buying fresh shucked oysters, look for a plump, moist oyster. The flesh should be creamy with a clear liquid (oyster liquor) surrounding it. Oysters should smell like the fresh sea and have no traces of shell particles. If you prefer to shuck the oysters yourself, look for tightly closed, unbroken shells. Oysters are often served on a bed of rock salt or crushed ice to help them remain stable and upright, and to keep them cool in summer.

INGREDIENTS

600 g (1¼ lb) chicken breast fillets
4 large spring onions
1 small green capsicum (pepper)
1 small red capsicum (pepper)
¼ cup (60 ml/2 fl oz) olive oil
1 teaspoon freshly ground black pepper
½ teaspoon ground turmeric
1½ teaspoons ground coriander (cilantro)

Curry mayonnaise
¾ cup (185 g/6 oz) whole-egg mayonnaise
1 tablespoon hot curry powder
¼ cup (60 g/2 oz) sour cream
1 tablespoon sweet fruit or mango chutney, mashed
¼ cup (45 g/1½ oz) peeled, finely chopped cucumber
½ teaspoon toasted cumin seeds
1 tablespoon finely chopped fresh mint
1 teaspoon finely chopped fresh mint, extra

1   Preheat a barbecue grill or flatplate to high. Trim the chicken of excess fat and sinew. Cut the chicken into 3 cm (1¼ inch) cubes. Cut the spring onions into 3 cm (1¼ inch) lengths. Cut the red and green capsicum into 3 cm (1¼ inch) squares.

2   Thread the chicken, spring onion and capsicum onto skewers. Arrange the kebabs, side by side, in a shallow, non-metal dish. Combine the oil, pepper, turmeric and coriander in a jug. Pour over the kebabs and place in the refrigerator to marinate for 30 minutes.

3   To make the curry mayonnaise, combine the mayonnaise, curry powder, sour cream, chutney, cucumber, cumin seeds and mint in a bowl, and mix well. Spoon the mixture into a dish or jug for serving and sprinkle with the extra chopped mint.

4   Lightly oil the hot barbecue grill or flatplate. Cook the kebabs for 2–3 minutes each side, or until cooked through and tender. Serve with the curry mayonnaise.

INGREDIENTS

4 eggs
$^1/_3$ cup (80 ml) thick (double) cream
4 tablespoons finely chopped fresh chives
1 tablespoon olive oil
40 g butter, melted
3 slices white bread
$^1/_4$ cup (60 g) sour cream
100 g ocean trout caviar or salmon roe
chopped fresh chives, to garnish

1   Whisk together one egg, 1 tablespoon of the cream and 1 tablespoon of the chopped
     chives, and season with salt and cracked black pepper. Pour into a 25 cm (10 inch)
     lightly greased non-stick frying pan and cook over medium heat on one side for 3 minutes,
     or until just set; the omelettes will be difficult to roll if cooked for too long. Turn out onto
     a sheet of baking paper. Repeat with the remaining eggs and cream until you have
     four omelettes.

2   Tightly roll one omelette into a neat roll, then take another omelette and wrap it around the
     first. Repeat with the remaining omelettes so that you have two rolls. Wrap separately in
     plastic wrap and refrigerate for 1 hour.

3   Meanwhile preheat the oven to moderate 180°C (350°F/Gas 4). Combine the oil and
     butter. Using a 3 cm (1$^1/_4$ inch) cutter, cut 24 rounds from the bread and brush with the
     butter and oil mixture. Place on a baking tray and bake for 20–30 minutes, or until crisp
     and golden. Allow to cool.

4   Cut each of the cooled omelette rolls into 12 rounds. Spread $^1/_2$ teaspoon of the sour
     cream onto each croûton, and sit a round of omelette on top. Top with a teaspoon of
     salmon roe and garnish with chopped chives.

INGREDIENTS

2 tablespoons oil
1 onion, chopped
2 garlic cloves, crushed
1 tablespoon ground cumin
3 teaspoons ground coriander (cilantro)
1 teaspoon chilli powder
400 g lean minced (ground) beef
375 g (1 1/2 cups) bottled tomato pasta sauce
425 g (15 oz) can refried beans
225 g (8 oz) packet plain corn chips
250 g (2 cups) grated Cheddar cheese, at room temperature
150 g (2/3 cup) sour cream
4 spring onions (scallions), green parts included, sliced
coriander (cilantro) leaves, to garnish

Guacamole
2 large, ripe avocados
1/2 small onion, grated
1–2 Jalapeño or serrano chillies, seeded and finely chopped
  (optional)
1 garlic clove, crushed
1 tomato, peeled, seeded and diced
1 tablespoon lime juice
2 tablespoons chopped coriander (cilantro) leaves

1 Preheat the oven to 180°C (350°F/Gas 4). Heat the oil in a large frying pan over medium heat and cook the onion, garlic, cumin, ground coriander and chilli powder for 2–3 minutes. Add the mince and cook over high heat for 3–4 minutes, or until well browned, breaking up any lumps with a fork. Stir in the tomato pasta sauce and refried beans and simmer for 10 minutes until the mixture thickens.

2 Meanwhile, to make the guacamole, cut the avocados in half and remove the stones. Scoop out the flesh, place in a small bowl and mash roughly with a fork. Add the onion, chilli (if using), crushed garlic, tomato, lime juice, chopped coriander and 1/4 teaspoon salt and stir until well combined.

3 Divide the corn chips among four serving plates (ovenproof), arranging them close together, with a slight well in the centre. Put in the oven for 10 minutes, or until the corn chips are hot and golden. Remove and sprinkle with the grated cheese (the heat from the chips will melt the cheese). Spoon equal quantities of the beef mixture into the well of each pile of chips. Top with the guacamole and sour cream and sprinkle with the spring onion. Garnish with coriander leaves.

INGREDIENTS

1 tablespoon olive oil
1 onion, finely chopped
large pinch allspice
1 teaspoon ground cumin
large pinch ground nutmeg
2 bay leaves
1 large head of cabbage
500 g (1 lb) minced (ground) lamb
1 cup (220 g/7 oz) short-grain white rice
4 cloves garlic, crushed
⅓ cup (50 g/1¾ oz) toasted pine nuts
2 tablespoons finely chopped fresh mint
2 tablespoons finely chopped fresh flat-leaf parsley
1 tablespoon finely chopped raisins
1 cup (250 ml/8 fl oz) olive oil, extra
⅓ cup (80 ml/2¾ fl oz) lemon juice
extra virgin olive oil, to drizzle
lemon wedges, to serve

1 Heat the oil in a saucepan, add the onion and cook over medium heat for 10 minutes, or until golden. Add the allspice, cumin and nutmeg, and cook for 2 minutes, or until fragrant. Remove from the pan.

2 Bring a very large saucepan of water to the boil and add the bay leaves. Remove the tough outer leaves and about 5 cm (2 inch) of the core from the cabbage with a sharp knife, then place the cabbage into the boiling water. Cook for 5 minutes, then carefully loosen a whole leaf with tongs and remove. Continue to cook and remove the leaves until you reach the core. Drain, reserving the cooking liquid, and set aside to cool.

3 Take 12 equal-size leaves and cut a small 'v' from the core end of each leaf to remove the thickest part, then trim the firm central veins so that the leaf is as flat as possible. Place three-quarters of the remaining leaves into a very large saucepan to prevent the rolls catching on the base.

4 Combine the mince, onion mixture, rice, garlic, pine nuts, mint, parsley and raisins in a bowl, and season well. With the core end of the leaf closest to you, shape 2 tablespoons of the mince mixture into an oval and place in the centre of the leaf. Roll up, tucking in the sides to enclose the filling. Repeat with the other 11 leaves and filling. Place the rolls tightly in a single layer in the saucepan, seam-side-down.

5 Combine 2½ cups (625 ml/20 fl oz) of the cooking liquid with the extra olive oil, lemon juice and 1 teaspoon salt, and pour over the rolls (the liquid should just cover the rolls). Top with the remaining leaves. Cover and bring to the boil, then reduce the heat and simmer for 1 hour 15 minutes, or until the filling is cooked. Remove from the pan and drizzle with extra virgin olive oil. Serve with lemon wedges.

INGREDIENTS

1 kg (2 lb) squid tubes, halved lengthways
1 cup (250 ml/8 fl oz) lemon juice
2 cups (250 g/8 oz) cornflour (cornstarch)
1¹/₂ tablespoons salt
1 tablespoon ground white pepper
2 teaspoons caster sugar
4 egg whites, lightly beaten
oil, for deep-frying
lemon wedges, for serving
fresh coriander (cilantro) leaves, to garnish

1   Open out the squid tubes, wash and pat dry. Lay on a chopping board with the inside facing upwards. Score a fine diamond pattern on the squid, being careful not to cut all the way through. Cut into pieces about 5 x 3 cm (2 x 1¹/₄ inches). Place in a flat non-metallic dish and pour the lemon juice over. Cover and refrigerate for 15 minutes. Drain and pat dry.

2   Combine the cornflour, salt, pepper and sugar in a bowl. Dip the squid into the egg white and dust with the flour mixture, shaking off any excess. Fill a deep heavy-based pan one third full of oil and heat to 180°C (350°F), or until a cube of bread dropped into the oil turns golden brown in 15 seconds. Deep-fry the squid, in batches, for 1–2 minutes, or until the squid turns white and curls. Drain on crumpled paper towels. Serve immediately.

INGREDIENTS

740 g can kidney beans, drained
1 teaspoon ground cumin
2 tablespoons olive oil
$^{1}/_{4}$ teaspoon cayenne pepper
1 avocado
1 small clove garlic, crushed
2 tablespoons sour cream
2 tablespoons lime juice
1 vine-ripened tomato, seeded and finely chopped
2 tablespoons finely chopped fresh coriander (cilantro)
250 g (9 oz) packet round tortilla chips

1   To make the refried beans, put the kidney beans in a bowl and mash well with a potato masher, then add the cumin. Heat $1^{1}/_{2}$ tablespoons of oil in a large non-stick frying pan and add the cayenne pepper and mashed kidney beans. Cook over medium– high heat for 2–3 minutes, stirring constantly. Allow to cool, then refrigerate for about 30 minutes, or until cold.

2   Scoop the avocado flesh into a food processor and add the garlic, sour cream and 1 table-spoon of the lime juice. Process for a few minutes until it is a thick creamy paste, then add salt to taste. Refrigerate.

3   To make the salsa, mix together the tomato, coriander and the remaining olive oil and lime juice in a bowl. Refrigerate until needed.

4   To assemble, lay out 36 round tortilla chips. Put a heaped teaspoon of refried beans in the centre of each chip, add a teaspoon of the avocado cream and lastly half a teaspoon of tomato salsa.

INGREDIENTS

3 cups (450 g/14 oz) char sui pork bun flour
1 cup (250 ml/8 fl oz) milk
1/2 cup (125 g/4 oz) caster sugar
1 tablespoon oil

Filling

2 teaspoons oil
1 clove garlic, crushed
2 spring onions, finely chopped
3 teaspoons cornflour (cornstarch)
2 teaspoons hoisin sauce
1 1/2 teaspoons soy sauce
1/2 teaspoon caster sugar
150 g (5 oz) Chinese barbecued pork, finely chopped

1   Set aside two tablespoons of flour. In a small pan, combine the milk and sugar and stir over low heat until dissolved. Sift the remaining flour into a large bowl and make a well in the centre. Gradually add the milk, stirring until it just comes together. Lightly dust a work surface with some of the reserved flour. Turn out the dough and knead for 10 minutes, or until smooth and elastic. Gradually incorporate the tablespoon of oil by kneading it into the dough a little at a time, kneading for about 10 minutes. Cover with plastic wrap and refrigerate for 30 minutes.

2   For the filling, heat the oil in a pan, add the garlic and spring onion and stir over medium heat until just soft. Blend the cornflour with 1/3 cup (80 ml/2 3/4 fl oz) water, the sauces and sugar and add to the pan. Stir over medium heat until the mixture boils and thickens, remove from the heat and stir in the pork. Allow to cool.

3   Divide the dough into 24 portions and flatten slightly, making the edges slightly thinner than the centre. Place teaspoons of filling in the centre of each and pull up the edges around the filling to enclose, pinching firmly to seal. Place each bun on a small square of greaseproof paper and place 3 cm (1 1/4 inches) apart on a bamboo or metal steamer. Place over a large pan of simmering water and steam in batches for 15 minutes, or until the buns have risen and are cooked through.

NOTE   Char sui pork bun flour is available at Asian food stores.

INGREDIENTS

$^1/_2$ cup (90 g/3 oz) roasted peanuts

$^1/_4$ cup (60 ml/2 fl oz) coconut milk

2 tablespoons lime juice

$^1/_2$ teaspoon ground turmeric

$^1/_4$ cup (60 ml/2 fl oz) oil

3 eggs, lightly beaten

125 g (4 oz) dried rice vermicelli

3 cloves garlic, crushed

1 tablespoon finely chopped fresh ginger

2 teaspoons shrimp paste (blachan)

6 spring onions, thinly sliced

400 g (13 oz) can baby corn, drained, quartered lengthways

150 g (5 oz) bean shoots

500 g (1 lb) Chinese cabbage, hard stems removed, thinly sliced

$^1/_2$ small red capsicum (pepper), thinly sliced

10 g ($^1/_4$ oz) fresh coriander (cilantro) leaves

$1^1/_2$ tablespoons fish sauce

2–3 large banana leaves, for serving

$^1/_2$ cup (90 g/3 oz) roasted peanuts, extra, chopped, to garnish

lime wedges, for serving

1 Mix the peanuts, coconut milk, lime juice and turmeric in a food processor until combined, but so the peanuts are only roughly chopped.

2 Heat 1 tablespoon of the oil in a large wok. Add the eggs and tilt the uncooked egg to the outside edge of the wok. Cook until firm, then remove from the wok and roll up firmly. Cut into thin slices.

3 Place the vermicelli in a bowl, cover with boiling water and soak for 5 minutes. Drain and cut into short lengths with scissors.

4 Heat the remaining oil in the wok. Add the garlic, ginger and shrimp paste and stir-fry for 30 seconds, or until aromatic. Add the vegetables and stir-fry until tender. Add the vermicelli and stir-fry until heated through. Stir in the peanut mixture and stir-fry until well combined and heated through. Turn off the heat and gently stir in the omelette and coriander leaves and fish sauce.

5 Cut the banana leaves into 11 cm ($4^1/_2$ inch) squares and blanch them in hot water for 10–15 seconds. Hold one corner of a square down on a flat surface with your finger, then fold one side of the banana leaf across, overlapping it into a cone shape. Secure down the side through to the base with a toothpick. Repeat to make 35 cones.

6 Spoon the filling into the cones, sprinkle with the extra peanuts and serve with lime wedges.

NOTE Banana leaves are available in the fruit and vegetable section of most supermarkets or in Asian or Pacific Island stores.

INGREDIENTS

2 cups (250 g/9 oz) plain flour
125 g (4¹/₂ oz) chilled butter, chopped
1 egg

Filling
¹/₄ cup (60 ml) lime juice
1 tablespoon fish sauce
1 tablespoon grated palm sugar or soft brown sugar
300 g fresh crab meat, shredded and well drained
2 tablespoons chopped fresh coriander (cilantro) leaves
1 tablespoon chopped fresh Vietnamese mint
1 small fresh red chilli, finely chopped
2 kaffir lime (makrut) leaves, finely shredded

1 Preheat the oven to moderately hot 200°C (400°F/Gas 6). Lightly grease 30 mini muffin holes. Sift the flour into a bowl and rub the butter in with your fingertips until the mixture resembles fine breadcrumbs. Make a well in the centre, add the egg and mix with a flat-bladed knife, using a cutting action until it comes together in beads. If the dough seems too dry, add a little cold water. Press the dough into a ball on a lightly floured surface, then wrap it in plastic wrap and refrigerate for 30 minutes.

2 Roll out the dough between two sheets of baking paper to 2 mm thick and cut out 30 rounds with a 6 cm (2¹/₂ inch) cutter. Press a round into each muffin hole. Prick the bases with a fork and bake for 6–8 minutes, or until golden. If they puff up, use a clean tea towel to press out any air pockets. Cool.

3 Combine the lime juice, fish sauce and sugar in a bowl and stir until the sugar is dissolved. Mix in the rest of the ingredients, then spoon into the prepared pastry cases and serve.

THAI-STYLE CRAB TARTLETS

TOFU BURGERS

1 tablespoon olive oil
1 red onion, finely chopped
200 g (6½ oz) Swiss brown mushrooms, finely chopped
350 g (11 oz) hard tofu (see note)
2 large cloves garlic
3 tablespoons chopped fresh basil
2 cups (200 g/6½ oz) dry wholemeal breadcrumbs
1 egg, lightly beaten
2 tablespoons balsamic vinegar
2 tablespoons sweet chilli sauce
1½ cups (150 g/5 oz) dry wholemeal breadcrumbs, extra
olive oil, for shallow-frying
6 wholemeal or wholegrain bread rolls
½ cup (125 g/4 oz) mayonnaise
100 g (3½ oz) semi-dried (sun-blushed) tomatoes
60 g (2 oz) rocket leaves
sweet chilli sauce, to serve

1 Heat the oil in a frying pan and cook the onion over medium heat for 2–3 minutes, or until soft. Add the mushrooms and cook for a further 2 minutes. Cool slightly.

2 Blend 250 g (8 oz) of the tofu with the garlic and basil in a food processor until smooth. Transfer to a large bowl and stir in the onion mixture, breadcrumbs, egg, vinegar and sweet chilli sauce. Grate the remaining tofu and fold through the mixture, then refrigerate for 30 minutes. Divide the mixture into six and form into patties, pressing together well. Coat them in the extra breadcrumbs.

3 Heat 1 cm (½ inch) oil in a deep frying pan and cook the patties in two batches for 4–5 minutes each side, or until golden. Turn carefully to prevent them breaking up. Drain on crumpled paper towels and season with salt.

4 Halve the bread rolls and toast under a hot grill. Spread mayonnaise over both sides of each roll. Layer semi-dried tomatoes, a tofu patty and rocket leaves in each roll and drizzle with sweet chilli sauce.

ARANCINI

440 g (2 cups) risotto rice (arborio, vialone nano or carnaroli)
1 egg, lightly beaten
1 egg yolk
50 g ('/₂ cup) grated Parmesan cheese
plain (all-purpose) flour
2 eggs, lightly beaten
dry breadcrumbs, to coat
oil, for deep-frying

Meat sauce
1 dried porcini mushroom
1 tablespoon olive oil
1 onion, chopped
125 g (4'/₂ oz) minced (ground) beef or veal
2 slices prosciutto, finely chopped
2 tablespoons tomato paste (purée)
80 ml ('/₃ cup) white wine
'/₂ teaspoon dried thyme leaves
3 tablespoons finely chopped parsley

1 Cook the rice in boiling water for 20 minutes, or until just soft. Drain, without rinsing and cool. Put in a large bowl and add the egg, egg yolk and Parmesan. Stir until the rice sticks together. Cover and set aside.

2 To make the meat sauce, soak the porcini in hot water for 10 minutes, then squeeze dry and chop finely. Heat the oil in a frying pan. Add the mushroom and onion and cook for 3 minutes, or until soft. Add the mince and cook, stirring, until browned. Add the prosciutto, tomato paste, wine, thyme and pepper to taste. Cook, stirring, for 5 minutes, or until all the liquid is absorbed. Stir in the parsley and set aside to cool. With wet hands, form the rice mixture into 10 balls. Wet your hands again and gently pull the balls apart. Place 3 teaspoons of the meat sauce in the centre of each. Reshape to enclose the filling. Roll in the flour, beaten egg and breadcrumbs and chill for 1 hour.

3 Fill a deep heavy-based pan one-third full of oil and heat to 180°C (350°F), or until a cube of bread browns in 15 seconds. Deep-fry the croquettes, two at a time, for 3–4 minutes, or until golden. Drain on paper towels and keep warm while cooking the rest.

850 g (1 lb 12 oz) cap mushrooms
40 g (1¹/₄ oz) butter
1 small onion, finely chopped
100 g (3¹/₂ oz) minced (ground) pork
60 g (2 oz) chorizo sausage, finely chopped
1 tablespoon tomato paste (tomato purée)
2 tablespoons dry breadcrumbs
1 tablespoon chopped fresh flat-leaf parsley

1 Remove the stalks from the mushrooms, then finely chop the stalks. Set aside.

2 Melt the butter in a frying pan over low heat, add the onion and cook, stirring occasionally, for 5 minutes, or until soft. Increase the heat to high, add the pork mince, and cook for 1 minute, stirring constantly and breaking up any lumps. Add the mushroom stalks and chorizo and continue cooking for 1 minute, or until the mixture is dry and browned. Add the tomato paste and ¹/₂ cup (125 ml/4 fl oz) water. Bring to the boil, then reduce the heat to low and simmer for 5 minutes, or until thick. Stir in the breadcrumbs, then transfer to a bowl and cool.

3 Preheat the oven to hot 210°C (415°F/Gas 6–7). Lightly grease a baking tray. Spoon about 1¹/₂ teaspoons of the cooled meat into the mushroom caps, smoothing the top with a flat-bladed knife so that the filling is slightly domed. Place on the tray and bake in the top half of the oven for 10 minutes. Sprinkle with the parsley and serve hot.

STUFFED MUSHROOMS

INGREDIENTS

1 cup (125 g/4^1/$_2$ oz) self-raising flour
2 eggs, lightly beaten
^{1}/$_2$ cup (125 ml/4^1/$_4$ fl oz) milk
2 tablespoons finely chopped fresh parsley
2 teaspoons finely chopped fresh sage

Pear and blue cheese topping
100 g (3^1/$_2$ oz) Blue Castello or other creamy blue cheese
75 g (2^1/$_2$ oz) cream cheese
2 teaspoons brandy
1 large ripe green-skinned pear
^{1}/$_4$ cup (30 g/1 oz) toasted walnuts, finely chopped
^{1}/$_2$ lemon
30 g (1 oz) chives, cut into 3–4 cm (1–2 inch) lengths

1   Sift the flour into a bowl and make a well in the centre. Gradually add the combined eggs and milk, mixing the flour in slowly. When the flour is incorporated, add the parsley and sage and season well. Whisk until a smooth batter forms.

2   Heat a large non-stick frying pan over medium heat and spray with cooking oil spray. Drop heaped teaspoons of batter into the pan and flatten them to give 5 cm (2 inch) circles. Cook until bubbles appear in the surface of the pikelet, then turn and brown the other side. Lift out to cool on a wire rack.

3   To make the topping, beat the cheeses and brandy together until smooth. Season with pepper. Cut the pear in half and peel and core one half, then dice it into 5 mm (^{1}/$_4$ inch) pieces, leaving the other half untouched. Stir the diced pear and walnuts into the cheese mixture. Core the other half of the pear but do not peel it. Thinly slice the pear lengthways. Cut each slice into 2 cm (1 inch) triangles with green skin on one side. Squeeze some lemon juice over the cut surfaces to prevent discoloration.

4   Spread 1 teaspoon of topping on each pikelet. Arrange three pear triangles on top and garnish with chives.

INGREDIENTS

1/2 cup (125 ml/4 fl oz) olive oil
6 spring onions, chopped
3/4 cup (150 g/5 oz) long-grain rice
1/4 cup (15 g/1/2 oz) chopped fresh mint
2 tablespoons chopped fresh dill
2/3 cup (170 ml/51/2 fl oz) lemon juice
1/4 cup (35 g/11/4 oz) currants
1/4 cup (40 g/11/4 oz) pine nuts
240 g (71/2 oz) packaged vine leaves (about 50)
2 tablespoons olive oil, extra

1 Heat the oil in a medium pan. Add the spring onion and cook over medium heat for 1 minute. Stir in the rice, mint, dill, half the lemon juice, and season, to taste. Add 1 cup (250 ml/8 fl oz) water and bring to the boil, then reduce the heat, cover and simmer for 20 minutes. Remove the lid, fork through the currants and pine nuts, cover with a paper towel, then the lid and leave to cool.

2 Rinse the vine leaves and gently separate. Drain, then dry on paper towels. Trim any thick stems with scissors. Line the base of a 20 cm (8 inch) pan with any torn or misshapen leaves. Choose the larger leaves for filling and use the smaller leaves to patch up any gaps.

3 Place a leaf shiny-side-down. Spoon a tablespoon of filling into the centre, bring in the sides and roll up tightly from the stem end. Place seam-side-down, with the stem end closest to you, in the base of the pan, arranging them close together in a single layer.

4 Pour in the rest of the lemon juice, the extra oil and about 3/4 cup (185 ml/6 fl oz) water to just cover the dolmades. Cover with an inverted plate and place a tin on the plate to firmly compress the dolmades and keep them in place while they are cooking. Cover with the lid.

5 Bring to the boil, then reduce the heat and simmer for 45 minutes. Cool in the pan. Serve at room temperature.

NOTE Store, covered with the cooking liquid, in the refrigerator for up to 2 weeks.

FRIED WHITEBAIT

500 g (1 lb) whitebait
2 teaspoons sea salt
$1/3$ cup (40 g/$1\frac{1}{4}$ oz) plain (all-purpose) flour
$1/4$ cup (30 g/1 oz) cornflour (cornstarch)
2 teaspoons finely chopped fresh flat-leaf parsley
olive oil, for deep-frying
1 lemon, cut into wedges, for serving

1   Combine the whitebait and sea salt in a bowl and mix well. Cover and refrigerate.

2   Combine the sifted flours and chopped parsley in a bowl and season well with cracked pepper. Fill a deep heavy-based pan one third full of oil and heat to 180°C (350°F), or until a cube of bread browns in 15 seconds. Toss a third of the whitebait in the flour mixture, shake off the excess and deep-fry for $1\frac{1}{2}$ minutes, or until pale and crisp. Remove with a slotted spoon and drain well on crumpled paper towels. Repeat with the remaining whitebait, cooking in two batches.

3   Reheat the oil and fry the whitebait a second time in three batches for 1 minute each, or until lightly browned. Drain on crumpled paper towels and serve hot with lemon wedges.

CRUMBED SHRIMP WITH PONZU DIPPING SAUCE

18 raw large prawns (jumbo shrimp)
2 tablespoons cornflour (cornstarch)
3 eggs
3 cups (240 g/8^1/$_2$ oz) fresh breadcrumbs
oil, for pan-frying
^{1}/$_3$ cup (80 ml/2^3/$_4$ fl oz) ponzu sauce or ^{1}/$_4$ cup (60 ml/2^1/$_4$ fl oz) soy sauce combined with 1 tablespoon lemon juice

1 Peel and devein the prawns, leaving the tails intact. Cut down the back of each prawn to form a butterfly. Place each prawn between two layers of plastic wrap and gently beat to form a cutlet.

2 Put the cornflour, eggs and breadcrumbs in separate bowls. Lightly beat the eggs. Dip each prawn first into the cornflour then into the egg and finally into the breadcrumbs, ensuring that each cutlet is well covered in crumbs.

3 Heat the oil in a frying pan over medium heat until hot. Cook six prawn cutlets at a time for about 1 minute each side, or until the crumbs are golden—be careful they don't burn. Serve immediately with ponzu sauce.

NOTE Ponzu is a Japanese dipping sauce usually used for sashimi.

INGREDIENTS

Basic pastry cases
2 cups (250 g/9 oz) plain (all-purpose) flour
125 g (4¹/₂ oz) chilled butter, chopped
1 egg

4 eggs and 4 egg yolks
75 g (2¹/₂ oz) unsalted butter
4 tablespoons roe

1   Preheat the oven to moderately hot 200°C (400°F/Gas 6). Lightly grease 30 mini muffin
    holes. Sift the flour into a large bowl and rub the butter in with your fingertips until the
    mixture resembles fine breadcrumbs. Make a well in the centre, add the egg and mix with
    a flat-bladed knife, using a cutting action until it comes together in beads. If the dough
    seems too dry, add a little cold water. Press the dough into a ball on a lightly floured
    surface, then wrap it in plastic wrap and refrigerate for 30 minutes.

2   Roll out the dough between two sheets of baking paper to 2 mm thick and cut out 30
    rounds with a 6 cm (2 inch) cutter. Press a round into each muffin hole. Prick the bases
    with a fork and bake for 6–8 minutes, or until dry and golden. If they puff up, use a clean
    tea towel to press out the air. Cool.

3   Lightly beat the eggs and egg yolks together. Melt the butter over very low heat, then add
    the eggs and whisk slowly and constantly for 5–6 minutes, or until the mixture is thick and
    creamy but the eggs are not scrambled. Remove from the heat straight away and season
    to taste. Fill each pastry case with 1 teaspoon of the creamed egg mixture, then top with
    ¹/₂ teaspoon of roe before serving.

INGREDIENTS

200 g (7 oz) chicken breast fillet, roughly chopped
150 g (5¼ oz) mild pancetta, chopped
1 clove garlic, crushed
3 spring onions, chopped
2 tablespoons chopped fresh coriander (cilantro)
2 bird's eye chillies, seeded and finely chopped
1 teaspoon fish sauce
1 egg
1 teaspoon grated fresh ginger
375 g (13 oz) block frozen puff pastry
1 egg yolk
2 tablespoons sesame seeds
sweet chilli sauce, to serve
fresh coriander (cilantro), to serve

1 Preheat the oven to moderate 180°C (350°F/Gas 4). Put the chicken, pancetta, garlic, spring onion, coriander, chilli, fish sauce, whole egg and ginger in a food processor and process until just combined.

2 Roll out the pastry to an oblong 30 x 40 cm (12 x 16 inches). Cut in half lengthways. Take half the filling and, using floured hands, roll it into a long sausage shape and place along the long edge of one piece of pastry. Brush the edges with a little water and fold over, pressing down to seal. Place the sealed edge underneath. Repeat with the remaining pastry and filling.

3 Using a sharp knife, cut the sausage rolls into 3 cm lengths on the diagonal; discard the end pieces. Brush the tops with egg yolk, then sprinkle with sesame seeds. Bake for 15 minutes, or until golden. Serve with sweet chilli sauce and garnished with coriander.

INGREDIENTS

Dipping sauce
2 tablespoons light soy sauce
3 tablespoons rice vinegar

3 dried shiitake mushrooms
350 g (12 oz) raw prawns (shrimp), peeled and deveined
4 spring onions (scallions), chopped
60 g (2¼ oz) snow peas (mangetout), chopped
2 teaspoons finely chopped ginger
2 garlic cloves, crushed
15 g (½ cup) chopped coriander (cilantro) leaves
100 g (3½ oz) water chestnuts, chopped
1 teaspoon sesame oil
1 tablespoon light soy sauce
1 egg white
1 teaspoon cornflour (cornstarch)
300 g (10½ oz) fresh rice sheet noodles

1 To make the dipping sauce, combine the soy sauce and rice vinegar.

2 Cover the mushrooms with hot water and soak for 15 minutes. Drain, discard the stems and finely chop the caps.

3 Mince the prawns in a food processor. Add the mushrooms, spring onion, snow peas, ginger, garlic, coriander, water chestnuts, sesame oil, soy sauce and a pinch of salt. Add the egg white and cornflour and pulse until smooth.

4 Line a large bamboo steamer with baking paper and place over a wok of simmering water (ensure the base doesn't touch the water). Gently unfold the rice sheet noodle and cut into six 15 cm (6 inch) squares. Divide the filling between the six rice noodle squares and spread it out evenly over each. Roll firmly to form a log. Steam, covered, in a wok for 5 minutes. Cut each roll in half and serve with the sauce.

INGREDIENTS

Spicy tomato sauce
2–3 red chillies, chopped
1 red capsicum (pepper), diced
425 g (14 oz) can chopped tomatoes
2 cloves garlic, finely chopped
2 tablespoons soft brown sugar
1^1/$_2$ tablespoons cider vinegar

1 cup (125 g/4 oz) plain (all-purpose) flour
2 teaspoons baking powder
^{1}/$_2$ teaspoon chilli powder
^{1}/$_2$ teaspoon ground turmeric
1 teaspoon ground cumin
2 eggs, beaten
1 cup (60 g/2 oz) chopped fresh coriander (cilantro) leaves
4 onions, very thinly sliced
oil, for deep-frying

1 To make the sauce, combine all the ingredients with 3 tablespoons water in a saucepan. Bring to the boil, then reduce the heat and simmer for 20 minutes, or until the mixture thickens. Remove from the heat.

2 To make the bhajis, sift the flour, baking powder, spices and 1 teaspoon salt into a bowl and make a well in the centre. Gradually add the combined egg and 3 tablespoons water, whisking to make a smooth batter. Stir in the coriander and onion.

3 Fill a deep heavy-based saucepan one-third full of oil and heat until a cube of bread dropped into the oil browns in 15 seconds. Drop dessertspoons of the mixture into the oil and cook in batches for 90 seconds each side, or until golden. Drain on paper towels. Serve with the spicy tomato sauce.

1 teaspoon dried yeast
$^1/_2$ teaspoon sugar
2$^1/_2$ cups (310 g/10 oz) plain (all-purpose) flour
$^1/_3$ cup (80 ml/2$^3/_4$ fl oz) olive oil
400 g (13 oz) pontiac potatoes, unpeeled
2 tablespoons olive oil, extra
1 tablespoon fresh rosemary leaves

1   Place the yeast, sugar and $^1/_3$ cup (80 ml/2$^3/_4$ fl oz) water in a small bowl, cover and leave
    in a warm place until foamy.

2   Sift the flour and $^1/_4$ teaspoon salt into a large bowl. Make a well in the centre and stir in
    the yeast mixture, the oil and $^1/_3$ cup (80 ml/2$^3/_4$ fl oz) water; mix to a soft dough. Turn out
    onto a lightly floured surface and knead for 5 minutes, or until the dough is smooth and
    elastic. Place the dough in an oiled bowl, cover and leave in a warm place for about
    1 hour, or until the dough has doubled in size.

3   Preheat the oven to hot 220°C (425°F/Gas 7). Punch down the dough to expel the air.
    Turn out and knead for 1 minute, or until smooth. Divide into 48 portions and roll each
    portion to a 5 cm (2 inch) round. Place on lightly greased baking trays.

4   Cut the potatoes into slices. Cover each dough round with a slice of potato, leaving a 1 cm
    ($^1/_2$ inch) border. Brush the pizzettas with the extra olive oil and sprinkle with rosemary
    leaves and salt. Bake on the highest shelf in the oven for 12–15 minutes, or until the
    pastry is crisp and lightly browned. Serve immediately.

INGREDIENTS

20 small new potatoes
250 g (8 oz) ricotta cheese
35 g (1¼ oz) Cheddar, grated
25 g (¾ oz) Parmesan, shredded
oil, for spraying or brushing
15 g (½ oz) fresh chives, finely chopped, to garnish

1 Preheat the oven to moderately hot 200°C (400°F/Gas 6). Boil or steam the potatoes for 10 minutes, or until just tender when tested with a skewer (do not overcook or the potatoes will fall apart when you are preparing them). Drain well and cool completely.

2 Meanwhile, in a small bowl combine the ricotta, Cheddar and Parmesan. Season, to taste, and set aside.

3 Cut the cooled potatoes in half and use a melon baller to scoop out the flesh, leaving a 5 mm (¼ inch) border. Discard the flesh.

4 Lightly spray the potato halves with oil and bake on baking trays for 30–45 minutes, or until crisp and golden. Heat the grill to high.

5 Fill each potato shell with a teaspoon of the cheese mixture and grill for 5–8 minutes, or until the tops are lightly golden and the cheese has melted. Arrange on a serving dish and garnish each with chopped chives. Serve immediately.

24 raw medium prawns (shrimp)
1 teaspoon cornflour (cornstarch)
24 won ton wrappers
oil, for deep-frying
$1/_2$ cup (125 ml) sweet chilli sauce
1 tablespoon lime juice

1   Peel the prawns, leaving the tails intact. Pull out the dark vein from each back, starting at the head end.

2   Mix the cornflour with 1 teaspoon water in a small bowl. Fold each won ton wrapper in half to form a triangle. Cover them with a tea towel while you are working, to prevent them drying out. Wrap each prawn in a wrapper, leaving the tail exposed. Seal at the end by brushing on a little of the cornflour mixture, then pressing gently. Spread the wrapped prawns on a baking tray, cover with plastic wrap and refrigerate for 20 minutes.

3   Fill a deep heavy-based saucepan one-third full of oil and heat to 180°C (350°F), or until a cube of bread dropped into the oil browns in 15 seconds. Cook the prawns in batches for $1^1/_2$ minutes each batch, or until crisp, golden and cooked through. The cooking time may vary depending on the size of the prawns. Determine the correct time by cooking one prawn and testing it before continuing. Remove the prawns from the oil and drain on crumpled paper towels.

4   Stir the sweet chilli sauce and lime juice together in a small bowl. Serve with the prawns.

WON TON WRAPPED PRAWNS

INGREDIENTS

$^1/_2$ cup (125 ml/4$^1/_4$ oz) soy sauce
$^1/_3$ cup (80 ml/2$^3/_4$ oz) Chinese rice wine
2 cloves garlic, crushed
1 teaspoon finely grated fresh ginger
1 teaspoon sesame oil
225 g (8 oz) beef fillet, cut into 2 cm (1 inch) cubes
8 spring onions
2 tablespoons toasted sesame seeds

1   Combine the soy sauce, wine, garlic, ginger and oil, and pour over the beef. Marinate for 20 minutes. Drain, reserving the marinade.

2   Cut six of the spring onions into 24 x 3 cm (1 inch) pieces and thread a piece plus two meat cubes onto 24 skewers. Cook on a hot barbecue hotplate or chargrill pan for 5 minutes, or until cooked. Remove, sprinkle with sesame seeds and keep warm.

3   Put the reserved marinade in a saucepan and bring to the boil for 1 minute, then add 2 thinly sliced spring onions. Pour into a bowl and serve with the skewers.

INGREDIENTS

310 g (2¹/₂ cups) plain (all-purpose) flour
125 g (4¹/₂ oz) butter, chilled and chopped
150 g (5¹/₂ oz) round steak, finely chopped
1 small potato, finely chopped
1 small onion, finely chopped
1 small carrot, finely chopped
1–2 teaspoons Worcestershire sauce
2 tablespoons beef stock
1 egg, lightly beaten

1 Grease a baking tray. Place the flour, butter and a pinch of salt in a food processor and process for 15 seconds, or until crumbly. Add 4–5 tablespoons of water and process in short bursts until the mixture comes together (add more water if needed). Turn out onto a floured surface and form into a ball. Cover with plastic wrap and chill for 30 minutes. Preheat the oven to 210°C (415°F/Gas 6–7).

2 Mix together the steak, potato, onion, carrot, Worcestershire sauce and stock. Season well.

3 Divide the dough into six portions and roll out each to 3 mm (1/8 inch) thick. Using a 16 cm (6¹/₂ inch) diameter plate as a guide, cut out six circles. Divide the filling evenly and put in the centre of each pastry circle.

4 Brush the edges of each pastry round with beaten egg and form into a semi-circle. Pinch the edges to form a frill and place on the tray. Brush with the remaining beaten egg and bake for 10 minutes. Lower the heat to 180°C (350°F/Gas 4). Cook for 20–25 minutes, or until golden.

CORNED BEEF, PARSNIP AND MINT PATTIES

INGREDIENTS

2 parsnips, chopped
1 cup (100 g/3¹/₂ oz) dry breadcrumbs
200 g (6¹/₂ oz) piece cooked corned beef, finely chopped
1 egg yolk
¹/₄ small onion, finely chopped
20 g (³/₄ oz) fresh mint leaves, finely chopped
1 tablespoon lemon juice
3 teaspoons wholegrain mustard
2 tablespoons plain (all-purpose) flour
1 egg
1 tablespoon milk
¹/₄ cup (60 ml/2 fl oz) olive oil
¹/₂ cup (140 g/41/2 oz) spicy tomato chutney
24 small fresh mint leaves, to garnish

1. Cook the parsnip in a large pan of boiling water for 10 minutes, or until tender. Drain and mash until smooth. Set aside to cool.

2. Mix the parsnip with ¹/₃ cup 35 g (1¹/₄ oz) of the breadcrumbs, the corned beef, egg yolk, onion, mint, lemon juice, mustard and salt and freshly ground black pepper.

3. Shape into 24 patties, pressing firmly together. Dust with flour and shake off any excess. Dip into the combined egg and milk, then coat in the remaining breadcrumbs.

4. Heat the oil in a large frying pan over medium-low heat and cook the patties in batches for 2–3 minutes each side, or until golden brown and heated through. Drain on crumpled paper towels. Spoon 1 teaspoon of tomato chutney onto each patty and top with a mint leaf. Serve immediately.

INGREDIENTS

Hollandaise sauce
3 egg yolks
2 tablespoons lime or lemon juice
125 g (4 oz) butter, melted

6–8 slices bread
oil spray
24 quail eggs
250 g (8 oz) English spinach, trimmed

1   Preheat the oven to moderate 180°C (350°F/Gas 4). To make the hollandaise sauce, blend the yolks and juice in a food processor for 5 seconds, then gradually add the melted butter. Transfer to a bowl and refrigerate for about 30 minutes, until thickened.

2   Cut 24 rounds of bread with a 4 cm (1½ inch) cutter. Place on a baking tray, spray with oil and bake for 10 minutes. Turn over and bake for another 5 minutes, until dry and crisp.

3   Put about 2.5 cm (1 inch) water in a large non-stick frying pan and bring to simmering point. Reduce the heat so the water is not moving. Carefully crack the eggs into the water. Spoon a little water onto the top of the eggs as they cook, and when set, remove from the pan and drain on paper towels.

4   Steam or microwave the spinach for 2 minutes, or until wilted, then drain well. To assemble, put some spinach on the bread rounds, then top with egg and drizzle with hollandaise. Serve immediately.

NOTE   Quail eggs are available from speciality food stores or can be ordered from poultry shops. You can use bottled hollandaise. Any leftover hollandaise will keep in the refrigerator, covered, for up to five days.

POLENTA WEDGES WITH BOCCONCINI AND TOMATOES

1 tablespoon olive oil
1²/₃ cups (250 g/9 oz) polenta
³/₄ cup (75 g/2¹/₂ oz) grated Parmesan
2¹/₂ tablespoons ready-made pesto
150 g (5¹/₄ oz) bocconcini, thinly sliced
12 cherry tomatoes, cut into quarters
¹/₂ cup (15 g/¹/₂ oz) fresh basil, larger leaves torn

1 Lightly grease a 20 cm x 30 cm (8 inch x 12 inch) baking tin with the olive oil. Bring 1 litre (4 cups) lightly salted water to the boil in a saucepan. Once the water is boiling, add the polenta in a steady stream, stirring continuously to prevent lumps forming. Reduce the heat to very low and simmer, stirring regularly, for about 20–25 minutes, or until the polenta starts to come away from the side of the pan.

2 Stir the Parmesan into the polenta and season with salt and pepper. Spoon the polenta into the baking tray, smooth the top with the back of a wet spoon and leave for 1 hour, or until set.

3 Once the polenta has set, carefully tip it out onto a board and cut into 24 x 5 cm (2 inch) squares, then cut each square into two triangles. Chargrill the polenta in batches on a preheated chargrill pan for 2–3 minutes on each side, or until warmed through.

4 Spread each triangle with 1 teaspoon of the pesto, top with a slice of bocconcini and a tomato quarter. Season and grill for 1–2 minutes, or until the cheese is just starting to melt. Garnish with basil and serve immediately.

INGREDIENTS

125 g (4 oz) smoked salmon
2 teaspoons softened butter
1 small onion, chopped
1¹/₂ teaspoons horseradish cream
30 g (1 oz) soft butter, extra
3 teaspoons chopped tarragon
1 lime, cut into tiny wedges
red or black caviar, to garnish

Chive pikelets (griddle cakes)
¹/₂ cup (60 g/2 oz) self-raising flour
1 tablespoon coarsely chopped chives
1 egg yolk, lightly beaten
¹/₂ cup (125 ml/4 fl oz) milk

1   Roughly chop the salmon. Heat the butter in a small pan, add the onion and cook until soft. Put the smoked salmon, onion, horseradish cream and extra butter in a food processor. Season with salt and freshly ground black pepper and mix until smooth. Add the tarragon and process until the pâté is just combined.

2   For the pikelets, sift the flour and a pinch of salt into a bowl. Stir in the chives and make a well in the centre. Gradually whisk in the yolk and enough milk to form a smooth lump-free batter, the consistency of thick cream. Set aside for 15 minutes, then lightly grease a non-stick frying pan and drop teaspoons of the batter into the pan. When bubbles appear on the surface of the pikelets, turn them over and brown the other side. Transfer to a wire rack to cool. Repeat with the remaining batter.

3   Pipe or spread the pâté onto the pikelets, garnish with a slice of lime and some caviar.

CHIPOLATA SAUSAGES WITH HORSERADISH CREAM

INGREDIENTS

2 tablespoons virgin olive oil

2 red onions, cut into thin wedges

2 tablespoons dark brown sugar

3 teaspoons balsamic vinegar

100 g (3¹/₂ oz) spreadable cream cheese

1 tablespoon horseradish cream

12 chipolata sausages

12 par-baked mini bread rolls

100 g (3¹/₂ oz) rocket leaves, stalks removed

1 Preheat the oven to hot 220°C (425°F/Gas 7). Heat 1¹/₂ tablespoons olive oil in a small pan. Add the onion and 11/2 tablespoons water, cover, and cook over medium heat for about 10 minutes, stirring occasionally, until the onion is soft and starting to brown. Stir in the sugar and vinegar and cook, uncovered, for 3 minutes, or until thick. Season and keep warm.

2 Meanwhile, in a small bowl, mix the cream cheese and horseradish cream until smooth.

3 Heat the remaining oil in a large frying pan and cook the sausages in batches over medium-low heat for 6–8 minutes, or until brown and cooked. Remove; drain on crumpled paper towels.

4 Meanwhile, heat the bread rolls according to the manufacturer's instructions. When hot, slice vertically, three-quarters of the way through, and spread with the horseradish mixture. Fill the rolls with rocket and a sausage, then onion. Serve.

NOTE If you can't get chipolatas, you can use thin sausages and twist them through the centre.

1/4 cup (45 g/1 1/2 oz) cracked wheat (burghul)

4 pieces Lavash bread 30 x 23 cm (12 x 9 inch)

2 spring onions, thinly sliced

1 large tomato, seeded, finely chopped

1 small Lebanese cucumber, finely chopped

15 g (1/2 oz) fresh flat-leaf parsley, chopped

1 tablespoon lemon juice

1 tablespoon virgin olive oil

1 tablespoon olive oil

1 onion, finely chopped

1 clove garlic, crushed

2 teaspoons ground coriander (cilantro)

1 teaspoon cumin seeds

1/2 teaspoon ground cinnamon

250 g (8 oz) minced (ground) chicken

300 g (10 oz) can chickpeas, rinsed, drained and mashed

10 g (1/4 oz) fresh flat-leaf parsley, extra, chopped

10 g (1/4 oz) fresh mint leaves, chopped

2 tablespoons plain (all-purpose) flour

vegetable oil, for shallow-frying

1/4 cup (60 g/2 oz) Greek-style natural yoghurt

1 Soak the cracked wheat in hot water for 20 minutes. Slice the bread into thirds widthways, then cut in half. Keep the bread covered with a damp cloth to prevent it drying out. Cut some baking paper the same size as the bread. Roll the paper up around the bottom half of the bread to form a cone and secure. Twist at the bottom. You will need 24 bread cones.

2 Drain the wheat in a fine mesh sieve, pressing out as much water as possible. Transfer to a bowl and mix with the onion, tomato, cucumber, parsley, lemon juice and virgin olive oil. Season.

3 Heat the olive oil in a pan, add the onion and garlic and cook, stirring over medium-low heat, for 5 minutes, or until the onion is soft. Add the spices and cook for another minute, or until the spices are aromatic.

4 Place the onion mixture, chicken mince, chickpeas, parsley and mint in a bowl, season with salt and pepper and mix until combined. Shape into 24 patties, pressing firmly together. Toss in the flour and shake off the excess.

5 Fill a deep, heavy-based pan one third full of oil and heat to 180°C (350°F), or until a cube of bread dropped into the oil turns golden brown in 15 seconds. Cook the felafels in batches for 3–4 minutes each side, or until golden and heated through. Drain on crumpled paper towels.

6 To assemble, place a felafel in each bread cone, top with tabbouli, then 1/2 teaspoon yoghurt.

CHICKEN FALAFEL WITH TABBOULI CONES

INGREDIENTS

500 g (1 lb) firm white fish fillets, skin removed
1½ tablespoons red curry paste
¼ cup (60 g/2 oz) sugar
¼ cup (60 ml/2 oz) fish sauce
1 egg
100 g (3½ oz) snake beans, thinly sliced
10 fresh kaffir lime (makrut) leaves, finely chopped
oil, for deep-frying

Dipping sauce
½ cup (125 g/4½ oz) sugar
¼ cup (60 ml/2 fl oz) white vinegar
1 tablespoon fish sauce
1 small fresh red chilli, chopped
2 tablespoons finely chopped carrot
2 tablespoons peeled, seeded and finely chopped cucumber
1 tablespoon roasted peanuts, chopped

1 Place the fish in a food processor and process until smooth. Add the curry paste, sugar, fish sauce and egg. Process for another 10 seconds, or until combined. Stir in the beans and chopped lime leaves.

2 Shape the mixture into walnut-size balls, then flatten them into patties.

3 Fill a wok one-third full of oil and heat to 180°C (350°F), or until a cube of bread dropped into the oil browns in 15 seconds. Cook in batches for 3–5 minutes, turning occasionally. Drain on crumpled paper towels.

4 To make the dipping sauce, place the sugar, vinegar, fish sauce, chilli and ½ cup (125 ml/ 4¼ fl oz) water in a saucepan. Simmer for 5 minutes, or until thickened slightly. Cool. Stir in the chopped carrot, cucumber and peanuts. Serve the dipping sauce with the fish cakes.

INGREDIENTS

8 thin slices prosciutto
45 g (1½ oz) fresh dill sprigs
75 g (2½ oz) pine nuts, toasted
60 g (2 oz) Parmesan, finely grated
2 cloves garlic, crushed
⅓ cup (80 ml/2¾ fl oz) virgin olive oil
1 French bread stick, sliced diagonally
2 teaspoons butter
7 eggs, lightly beaten
⅓ cup (80 ml/2¾ fl oz) milk

1 Preheat the oven to moderately hot 200°C (400°F/Gas 6). Spread the prosciutto on a baking tray lined with baking paper. Bake for 5 minutes, or until sizzling and lightly crisp. Set aside.

2 Finely chop the dill, pine nuts, Parmesan and garlic together in a food processor. With the motor running, add the oil in a thin stream and process until smooth. Season.

3 Arrange the bread on baking trays and grill until golden on both sides. Spread with dill pesto.

4 Heat the butter in a large non-stick frying pan over low heat. Add the combined eggs and milk. As the egg begins to set, use a wooden spoon to scrape along the base with long strokes to bring the cooked egg to the surface in large lumps. Repeat several times over 10 minutes, or until the mixture is cooked but still creamy-looking. Remove from the heat and stir in the sour cream. Season with salt and pepper.

5 Divide the egg among the toasts and top with torn prosciutto. Serve immediately.

IN ADVANCE: Pesto can be made 3 days ahead and refrigerated. Use at room temperature.

INGREDIENTS

2 tablespoons olive oil
2 onions, thinly sliced
$^1/_3$ cup (80 ml/2$^3/_4$ oz) dry white wine
3 teaspoons sugar
1 cup (30 g/1 oz) chopped fresh flat-leaf parsley
8 anchovies, drained and finely chopped
1 cup (130 g/4$^1/_2$ oz) coarsely grated Gruyère
6 sheets filo pastry
60 g (2 oz) unsalted butter, melted

1   Preheat the oven to hot 220°C (425°F/Gas 7) and warm a baking tray. Heat the oil in a
frying pan and cook the onion over low heat for 5 minutes. Add the wine and sugar, and
cook for 10–15 minutes, or until the onion is golden. Remove from the heat and cool.

2   Combine the parsley with the anchovies, cheese and cooled onion.

3   Keeping the filo covered while you work, take one sheet, brush lightly with the butter,
cover with another sheet and repeat until you have three buttered sheets. Spread the
parsley mixture over the pastry and top with the remaining three sheets, buttering each
layer as before. Press down firmly, then cut the pastry in half widthways, then cut each
half into strips 1.5–2 cm ($^1/_2$–1 inch) wide. Brush with butter, then gently twist each strip.
Lightly season with black pepper, place on a baking tray and bake for 10–15 minutes,
or until golden.

50 g unsalted butter
2 tablespoons orange juice
6 small–medium fresh figs
6 long thin slices of prosciutto, trimmed of excess fat
24 sage leaves

1 Place the butter in a small heavy-based saucepan. Melt over low heat, then cook the butter for 8–10 minutes, or until the froth subsides and the milk solids appear as brown specks on the bottom of the saucepan. Strain the butter into a clean bowl by pouring it through a strainer lined with a clean tea towel or paper towel. Stir the orange juice into the strained butter.

2 Gently slice the figs lengthways into quarters. Cut each slice of prosciutto into four even strips. Sit a sage leaf on each fig segment, then wrap a piece of prosciutto around the middle with the ends tucked under the bottom of the fig. Arrange the figs, cut-side-up, on a baking tray and brush lightly with the butter mixture.

3 Move the grill tray to its lowest position, then preheat the grill to hot. Place the baking tray of figs on the grill tray and grill the figs for 1–1$\frac{1}{2}$ minutes, or until the prosciutto becomes slightly crispy. Serve hot or at room temperature. If you are serving the figs hot, provide serviettes to avoid burnt fingers.

TOASTED FIGS IN PROSCIUTTO

INGREDIENTS

300 g (10$^1/_2$ oz) zucchini (courgette)
4 spring onions, thinly sliced
200 g (7 oz) haloumi cheese, coarsely grated
$^1/_4$ cup (30 g/1 oz) plain flour
2 eggs
1 tablespoon chopped fresh dill, plus sprigs, to garnish
$^1/_4$ cup (60 ml/2 fl oz) oil
1 lemon, cut into very thin slices, seeds removed
$^1/_3$ cup (90 g/3 oz) thick Greek-style yoghurt

1   Coarsely grate the zucchini and squeeze out as much liquid as possible in your hands or in a clean tea towel. Combine the zucchini with the spring onion, haloumi, flour, eggs and dill. Season well with salt and cracked black pepper.

2   Heat the oil in a large heavy-based frying pan. Form fritters (using heaped teaspoons of the mixture) and cook in batches for 2 minutes each side, or until golden and firm. Drain on crumpled paper towels.

3   Cut each slice of lemon into quarters or eighths, depending on the size, to make small triangles.

4   Top each fritter with $^1/_2$ teaspoon yoghurt, a piece of lemon and a small sprig of dill.

NOTE   The fritters are best prepared and cooked as close to the serving time as possible or the haloumi tends to go a little tough.

INGREDIENTS

Ginger and soy dipping sauce

2 cm x 2 cm (1 inch x 1 inch) piece fresh ginger, cut into
    julienne strips
2 tablespoons Japanese soy sauce
2 tablespoons mirin
1 teaspoon wasabi paste
$^{1}/_{4}$ teaspoon sesame oil

Tuna cubes

600 g (21 oz) fresh tuna steaks
1 teaspoon wasabi powder
$^{1}/_{3}$ cup (50 g/1$^{3}/_{4}$ oz) black sesame seeds
$^{1}/_{4}$ cup (60 ml/2 fl oz) oil

1   To make the dipping sauce, combine the ginger, Japanese soy sauce, mirin, wasabi paste
    and sesame oil.

2   Cut the tuna into 2 cm (1 inch) cubes using a very sharp knife. Toss with the combined
    wasabi powder and black sesame seeds until evenly coated.

3   Heat a wok over high heat, add half the oil and swirl to coat. Add half the tuna and cook,
    tossing gently, for 1–2 minutes, or until lightly golden on the outside but still pink in the
    middle. Drain on crumpled paper towels and repeat with the remaining oil and tuna.
    Arrange on a platter with dipping sauce in the centre and serve with toothpicks so that
    your guests can pick up the cubes.

SESAME AND WASABI-CRUSTED TUNA CUBES

INGREDIENTS

Dipping sauce
1/3 cup (80 ml/2 3/4 oz) tonkatsu sauce or barbecue sauce
2 tablespoons lemon juice
1 tablespoon sake or mirin
1–2 teaspoons grated fresh ginger

250 g (9 oz) dried somen noodles
3 sheets nori (dried seaweed)
1/2 cup (60 g/2 oz) plain (all-purpose) flour
2 egg yolks
24 raw medium prawns (shrimp), peeled and deveined with
    the tails intact
oil, for deep-frying

1   Combine the dipping sauce ingredients, adding the ginger to taste.

2   Using a sharp knife, cut the noodles to the same length as the prawns (from the head to
    the base of the tail). Keep the noodles in neat bundles. Cut the nori into 2.5 cm (1 inch)
    wide strips.

3   Sift the flour and make a well in the centre. Mix the egg yolks with 1/4 cup (60 ml/2 fl oz)
    of water. Gradually add to the flour, whisking to make a smooth batter. Add another
    tablespoon of water if the mixture is too thick.

4   Dip a prawn in the batter, letting the excess run off. Roll the prawn lengthways in noodles
    to coat it with a single layer. Keep the noodles in place by rolling a nori strip around the
    centre of the prawn and securing it with a little batter. Repeat with the rest of the prawns.

5   Fill a deep heavy-based saucepan or deep-fryer one-third full of oil and heat to 180°C
    (350°F), or until a cube of bread browns in 15 seconds. Deep-fry 2–3 prawns at a time,
    for about 1–2 minutes, or until the prawns are cooked. Drain on crumpled paper towels
    and keep warm. Serve warm with the dipping sauce.

1 tablespoon butter

4 spring onions, thinly sliced

1 egg

2 tablespoons sour cream

350 g (12 oz) fresh white crab meat, excess liquid
    squeezed out

1 small yellow capsicum (pepper), finely diced

2 teaspoons chopped fresh thyme

2^1/$_2$ cups (200 g/7 oz) fresh white breadcrumbs

olive oil, for shallow-frying

Coriander (cilantro) paste

1 clove garlic

1 green chilli, seeded

^{1}/$_2$ teaspoon ground cumin

^{1}/$_4$ teaspoon sugar

^{3}/$_4$ cup (25 g/^{3}/$_4$ oz) fresh coriander (cilantro) leaves

^{1}/$_2$ cup (10 g/^{1}/$_3$ oz) fresh mint

1 tablespoon lemon juice

25 ml (^{3}/$_4$ fl oz) coconut cream

^{1}/$_2$ avocado

1 Line a tray with baking paper. Melt the butter in a frying pan over low heat. When it begins to foam, add the spring onion and cook for 2 minutes, or until softened. Remove from the heat and cool.

2 Mix the egg and sour cream until just smooth. Add the spring onion, crab, capsicum, thyme and ^{1}/$_2$ cup (40 g/1^1/$_2$ oz) of the breadcrumbs, season and mix together. Shape the mixture into flat rounds, using 1 level tablespoon for each. Place on the tray and refrigerate for 30 minutes.

3 Meanwhile, to make the coriander paste, process the garlic, chilli, cumin, sugar, herbs, lemon juice and ^{1}/$_4$ teaspoon salt in a food processor until a fine paste forms. Add the coconut cream and continue to blend until smooth. Add the avocado and, using the pulse action, process until just smooth. Transfer to a bowl, cover with plastic wrap and chill.

4 Using your hands, coat the crab cakes in the remaining breadcrumbs. Heat enough olive oil in a non-stick frying pan to just coat the bottom. Cook in batches for 2–3 minutes each side, or until golden. Drain and serve warm with ^{1}/$_2$ teaspoon of coriander paste on each.

MINI CRAB CAKES WITH CILANTRO PASTE

INGREDIENTS

Basic pizza dough
10 g ($^1/_3$ oz) dried yeast
1 teaspoon caster sugar
4 cups (500 g) plain (all-purpose) flour
2 tablespoons olive oil

1 tablespoon olive oil, plus extra for brushing
375 g (13 oz) minced (ground) lamb
1 onion, finely chopped
$^1/_4$ cup (40 g/$1^1/_2$ oz) pine nuts
1 tomato, peeled, seeded and chopped
$^1/_4$ teaspoon ground cinnamon
pinch of allspice
2 teaspoons chopped fresh coriander (cilantro), plus extra
   for serving
2 teaspoons lemon juice
$^1/_4$ cup (60 g/2 oz) plain yoghurt

1   Combine the yeast, sugar and $^3/_4$ cup (185 ml) warm water. Cover and leave for 10 minutes, or until frothy. If it hasn't foamed after 10 minutes, discard and start again.

2   Sift the flour and $^1/_2$ teaspoon salt and make a well. Add the yeast mixture and oil. Mix with a flat-bladed knife, using a cutting action, until a dough forms. Knead for 10 minutes, or until smooth. Place in an oiled bowl, cover with plastic wrap and leave for 45 minutes, or until doubled in size.

3   Heat the oil in a frying pan over medium heat and cook the mince for 3 minutes, or until browned. Add the onion and cook over low heat for 8 minutes, or until soft. Add the pine nuts, tomato, spices, $^1/_4$ teaspoon cracked pepper and some salt. Cook for 8 minutes, or until dry. Stir in the coriander and lemon juice and season.

4   Preheat the oven to very hot 230°C (450°F/Gas 8). Punch down the dough, then knead for 8 minutes, or until elastic. Roll out into 24 ovals. Spoon some filling onto each base. Pinch together the two short sides to form a boat shape. Brush with oil, and place the pizzas on a greased baking tray. Bake for 10 minutes. Serve with a dab of yoghurt and some coriander.

20 dried bamboo leaves
125 ml ($^1/_2$ cup/$4^1/_4$ fl oz) oil
6 spring onions (scallions), chopped
400 g (14 oz) eggplant (aubergine), cut into 1 cm ($^1/_2$ inch) cubes
90 g ($3^1/_4$ oz) drained water chestnuts, chopped
1 tablespoon mushroom soy sauce
3 small red chillies, seeded and finely chopped
2 teaspoons sugar
3 tablespoons chopped coriander (cilantro) leaves
800 g (4 cups) white glutinous rice, washed and well drained
2 tablespoons soy sauce

1 Soak the bamboo leaves in boiling water for 10 minutes until soft. Drain.

2 Heat half the oil in a wok. Cook the spring onion and eggplant over high heat for 4–5 minutes, or until golden. Stir in the water chestnuts, soy sauce, chilli, sugar and coriander. Cool.

3 Bring 750 ml (3 cups) water to a simmer. Heat the remaining oil in a saucepan, add the rice and stir for 2 minutes. Stir in 125 ml ($^1/_2$ cup) of the hot water over low heat until it is absorbed. Repeat until all the water has been added (about 20 minutes). Add the soy sauce and season with white pepper.

4 Fold one end of a bamboo leaf on the diagonal to form a cone. Hold in one hand and spoon in 2 tablespoons of rice. Make an indent in the rice, add 1 tablespoon of eggplant filling, then top with 1 tablespoon of rice. Fold the other end of the leaf over to enclose the filling. Secure with a toothpick and tie tightly with string. Repeat with the remaining bamboo leaves, rice and filling. Place in a single layer inside a double bamboo steamer. Cover pand put over a wok half filled with simmering water. Steam for $1^1/_2$ hours, or until the rice is tender, adding more boiling water as needed. Serve hot.

STICKY RICE POCKETS

INGREDIENTS

2 sheets frozen puff pastry
300 g (10 oz) goats cheese, sliced
2 cooking apples
2 tablespoons extra virgin olive oil
1 tablespoon chopped fresh lemon thyme

1 Preheat the oven to hot 210°C (415°F/Gas 6–7). While the pastry is still frozen, cut each sheet into four squares and then each square into quarters. Place slightly apart on a lightly greased baking tray. Set aside for a few minutes to thaw and then lay the cheese over the centre of each square of pastry, leaving a small border.

2 Core the unpeeled apples and slice them thinly. Interleave several slices over the pastry, making sure the cheese is covered completely. Lightly brush the apples with oil and sprinkle with lemon thyme and a little salt and pepper, to taste.

3 Bake the tarts for 20–25 minutes, or until the pastry is cooked through and golden brown at the edges. The tarts are best served immediately.

INGREDIENTS

1 cup (125 g/4 oz) plain (all-purpose) flour
75 g (2¹/₂ oz) butter, chopped
1 tablespoon bottled green peppercorns, drained
1 egg yolk
1 teaspoon Dijon mustard

Sweet onion filling
2 tablespoons olive oil
3 onions, sliced
1 clove garlic, sliced
2 teaspoons sugar
2 tablespoons balsamic vinegar
3 tablespoons raisins
1 tablespoon olive paste
75 g (2¹/₂ oz) feta cheese

1 Lightly grease 20 holes in two 12-hole round-based patty tins. Sift the flour and ¹/₄ teaspoon salt into a bowl and add the butter. Rub in with your fingertips until the mixture resembles fine breadcrumbs. Make a well in the centre. Crush the peppercorns with the back of a knife and chop finely. Add to the flour with the egg yolk, mustard and up to 2 teaspoons water. Mix with a flat-bladed knife until the mixture comes together in beads. Turn onto a lightly floured surface and press together into a ball. Wrap in plastic wrap and refrigerate for 20 minutes.

2 Preheat the oven to moderately hot 200°C (400°F/Gas 6). Roll the dough out on a lightly floured surface to 2–3 mm (about ¹/₈ inch). Cut 20 rounds with an 8 cm (3 inch) cutter. Put in the patty tins and prick with a fork. Bake for 8–10 minutes, or until golden.

3 For the filling, heat the oil in a heavy-based pan. Add the onion and garlic and cook, covered, over low heat for 30 minutes, or until the onion is very soft and beginning to brown. Increase the heat to moderate, add the sugar and vinegar and cook, stirring, until most of the liquid has evaporated and the onion is glossy. Stir in the raisins.

4 Spread a little olive paste into the base of each pastry case. Spoon the onion mixture over it and crumble the feta cheese on top. Serve warm or at room temperature.

INGREDIENTS

2–3 young banana leaves, or foil
2 cups (400 g/13 oz) glutinous rice
³/₄ cup (185 ml/6 fl oz) coconut milk

Chicken filling
2 tablespoons oil
2–3 cloves garlic, crushed
6 curry leaves
1 teaspoon dried shrimp paste
2 teaspoons ground coriander (cilantro)
2 teaspoons ground cumin
¹/₂ teaspoon turmeric
250 g (8 oz) minced (ground) chicken
3 tablespoons coconut milk, extra
1 teaspoon lemon juice

1 With a sharp knife, cut away the central ribs of the banana leaves. The leaves will split into large pieces—cut into pieces about 15 cm (6 inches) square. Blanch in boiling water briefly to soften them, then spread out on a tea towel and cover.

2 Wash the rice, drain and put in a large heavy-based pan with 1³/₄ cups (440 ml/14 fl oz) water. Bring slowly to the boil, reduce the heat to very low, cover tightly and cook for 15 minutes.

3 Put the coconut milk and ¹/₂ cup (125 ml/4 fl oz) water in a small pan and heat without boiling. Stir through the rice with a fork. Transfer to a bowl and set aside to cool.

4 For the chicken filling, heat the oil in a large heavy-based frying pan, add the garlic and curry leaves and stir for 1 minute over medium heat. Add the shrimp paste, coriander, cumin and turmeric and cook for another minute. Add the chicken mince and cook and break up with a fork for 3–4 minutes, or until the chicken changes colour. Add the extra coconut milk and continue to cook over low heat for 5 minutes, or until absorbed. Remove the curry leaves. Add the lemon juice and salt and pepper, to taste. Cool.

5 Place 1 heaped tablespoon of rice in the centre of each piece of banana leaf and flatten to a 4 cm (1¹/₂ inch) square. Top with a heaped teaspoon of filling. Roll the leaf into a parcel and place, seam-side-down, in a steamer lined with leftover banana leaf scraps. Steam, in batches, for 15 minutes. Serve at room temperature with chopsticks or small forks.

NOTE Banana leaves are used throughout Asia to wrap foods for steaming or baking. They keep the food moist and impart a mild flavour. They can be bought at Asian food stores if you don't have access to fresh leaves from a plant.